180

HEALING

PRAYERS

for the WORLD

Inspiration &
Encouragement for Girls

Janice Thompson

BARBOUR kidz
A Division of Barbour Publishing

YOU CAN PRAY HEALING PRAYERS FOR THE WORLD

Sure, you're just a girl, but you can still change the world around you. Think about those words for a moment. No matter where you come from, where you live, what school you go to, or what grade you're in, God can use you to make a difference for eternity. Whether you have red hair and freckles, blue eyes or brown, you can stir things up (in a good way!) in the lives of those around you. God wants to use you. Yes, *you!* Isn't that cool? He says you're a world changer. Don't you love that? It's time to start seeing yourself as a girl who can bring change to the world. That's why this book was written: to help you pray. Check it out! Every day you'll find a new topic, a prayer, a scripture, and a "be the change" activity—something you can do to grow in your faith or to help others. (Note: some activities might require help from a grown-up!) Nothing can hold you back when you start to see yourself as a world changer. What are you waiting for? . . . Let's go!

RANDOM ACTS OF KINDNESS

But we do not want you to be uninformed, brothers,
about those who are asleep, that you may not
grieve as others do who have no hope.
1 THESSALONIANS 4:13 ESV

Random acts of kindness. They're so fun, Lord! I love dreaming up all sorts of ideas—things I can do to bless kids, grown-ups, friends, family members, or even strangers. Coaches, teachers, the clerk at the supermarket. . .I want to bless them all with unexpected encouragement and surprises. Elderly neighbors, coworkers, expectant moms. . . They all need Your touch and a reminder that they are not alone. I need Your help to come up with creative ideas. What a great time we're going to have—You and me—dreaming up cool things to let these amazing people know You haven't forgotten them. Let's get started, Lord! Amen.

. . . .

Be the Change
Surprise a stranger by complimenting them.

IN THE SAME WAY

*"In the same way, let your light shine before others,
so that they may see your good works and give
glory to your Father who is in heaven."*
MATTHEW 5:16 ESV

Lord, I know the only chance I have of making a real difference in this world is to follow the example of Your Son, Jesus. He stepped w-a-y outside of His comfort zone and approached people in practical ways. If they needed food, He made sure they had food. Yum! If they needed healing, He healed them. Amazing! Best of all, He took the time to get to know each person, to check out their needs before fixing their problem. That way, they truly felt cared for. Today, please point out someone I can help, a person who needs a little light in his or her life. I want to get to know that person, Lord. Maybe they need a friend like me. I want to be the hands and feet of Jesus to someone in need, I pray. Amen.

. . . .

Be the Change
*Give in a sacrificial way, as Jesus did, and offer
to clean out your parents' garage or attic.*

WORLD CHANGERS

*Again Jesus spoke to them, saying, "I am the light
of the world. Whoever follows me will not walk
in darkness, but will have the light of life."*
JOHN 8:12 ESV

I've been reading Bible stories of the lives You changed—Abram, Moses, David, Rahab, Jonah, and so many more. Whew! There's quite a list of world changers in there! Not all of these people were willing at first. I can't blame them for being scaredy-cats! I get a little nervous myself. But here's the cool part: You used every one of these people to change the world. They made a big difference in the lives of others wherever they went. I want to be like that, Lord! Today I choose to give up my fear (Oh, help!) and to look for those who are in need. Give me Your ears to hear and Your eyes to see. I want to shine brightly, Lord, but not in my own strength. May I never forget—You're the leader, Jesus. I'm the follower. Amen.

. . . .

Be the Change
*Ask a parent to take you to a local soup kitchen to volunteer.
You might just make a few friends along the way.*

PAY IT FORWARD

God looked at the light and saw that it was good.
He separated light from darkness.
GENESIS 1:4 CEV

One of the things I love most about You, Lord, is that You always pay it forward. You bless me, knowing I will want to bless others. How fun! It's like a little game we play. I come up with fun and random ideas to surprise people (just to bring a smile to their faces). They get excited and pay it forward by blessing someone else. I love this game! It's the gift that keeps on giving! Show me how to pay it forward every single day, in little ways and in big ones too. I want my life to be filled with adventure, overflowing with opportunities to bless others and share Your light as I go along. This is so exciting, Lord! I'm grateful to be used by You. Amen.

. . . .

Be the Change
Pay it forward—do a good deed for someone
that encourages them to pass it along.

YOUR BEST GIFT

*Light in a messenger's eyes brings joy to the heart,
and good news gives health to the bones.*
PROVERBS 15:30 NIV

I don't always feel like I have a lot to give, Lord. I don't have a lot of money, after all! Sometimes I even get a little sad thinking about this. I'm just a kid, but I want to do big things. Then I remember. . .You're not limited by money. There are a zillion ways I can impact the lives of those around me without spending a penny. I can send encouraging notes, offer to mow someone's lawn, even bless an elderly neighbor with the gift of a visit and some cookies. Today, please show me some creative, inexpensive ways I can reach out to my neighbors, my friends, elderly loved ones, and those in need. I can't wait to grab a pen and paper to make my list! Amen.

Be the Change
Visit with an elderly neighbor and ask them about their life.

A CITY ON A HILL

*"You are the light of the world. A town
built on a hill cannot be hidden."*
MATTHEW 5:14 NIV

Lord, one of the hardest things about being a Christian is this whole "shining bright" thing. I'm kind of shy sometimes. I don't want to draw attention to myself. It's embarrassing, especially when I'm hanging out with my friends who don't know You! Instead of shining like a city on a hill, I want to hide in the corner or keep my faith to myself. I get a little scared, if You want the truth. But You didn't create me to hide my light under a bushel. There are people out there who need glimpses of Your love, and You long for me to shine bright so that I can draw them to You. So, here I go, Lord! No more hiding for me. Ready, set, shine! Amen.

. . . .

Be the Change
*Why not host a sandwich-making party and have a parent
help you deliver your meals to the homeless? They will
appreciate it, and you'll have fun with the prep work.*

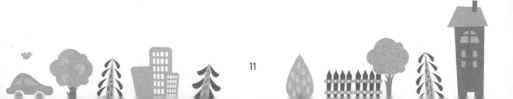

LIGHTING THE HOUSE

"No one lights a lamp and then puts it under a basket. Instead, a lamp is placed on a stand, where it gives light to everyone in the house."
MATTHEW 5:15 NLT

Wow, what a cool scripture, Lord! Even back in Bible times, people knew that lifting up the light would make it stretch farther. The lights in my house are mostly on the ceiling. I flip a switch and the room floods with light because the beams are shining down from above, spreading out over everything below. The whole room comes alive with light! That's how I want to be, Father, a bright light that draws people to You, not me. I don't want to hide myself away under a basket or bushel. May every deed, every action, flood lives with heavenly beams of light that point directly to You so that everyone might come to know You. Amen.

. . . .

Be the Change
Offer to do some yard work for a neighbor.

NOT OVERCOME

*The light shines in the darkness, and the
darkness has not overcome it.*
JOHN 1:5 NIV

So many people are struggling, Lord. It totally breaks my heart! Many are homeless. . .and hopeless. Some people are struggling from paycheck to paycheck, wondering if they'll make it. They don't have much food in the pantry. That makes me so sad! Other people have lost their jobs. That's really scary. Things can seem dark and gloomy. I might be a kid, but I can still make a difference in the lives of those who are going through tough stuff. I don't want people to be overwhelmed in their situations when I'm able to spread Your light through a kind deed or word. With Your help I want to come up with fun ideas to lift spirits and spread the joy. Thanks for the reminder that I can brighten the lives of people who feel like giving up. Amen.

. . . .

Be the Change
*Offer to share your skills in writing, art, or music
with another kid in class who may need the help.*

EARS WIDE OPEN!

"Then the righteous will shine like the sun in the kingdom of their Father. Whoever has ears, let them hear."
MATTHEW 13:43 NIV

I get it, Lord. You want me to keep my ears tuned in to Your still, small voice at all times—not just when I'm going through tough stuff. Sure, You give me instructions for my own life, but You also long for me to reach out to others and make their lives happier too. So, You give me little taps on the shoulder. You whisper, "That one. She's the one who needs your help this time." You're the one who pointed me in the direction of a friend at school who didn't have lunch money. You're the one who reminded me to ask my parents if they would help pay for another friend's high medical bills. You're the one who nudges me daily to pray for that teacher who's going through a rough time. I'm listening, Lord. Ears wide open. May I hear. . .and obey. Amen.

. . . .

Be the Change
Get to know a kid in your class who usually sits alone and offer your friendship.

ARISE, SHINE

"Arise, shine, for your light has come,
and the glory of the LORD rises upon you."
ISAIAH 60:1 NIV

It's hard to get moving when you've been still for so long. When I've been playing computer games or watching a TV show, I don't want to be bothered. No thanks! It's easier to stay glued to the chair. I say things like, "Someone else will take care of it," or "I'm too busy." Then I'm reminded of the life of Your Son, how—day after day—Jesus went out of His way to help those in need. He didn't waste time on games or TV shows. He healed the sick, talked to people about heaven, and shared love with everyone He met. Jesus kept going and going, even when He was tired. I want to learn from His example, Father. Today I choose to get up off the sofa so that I can impact this world for You. Amen.

. . . .

Be the Change
Have a parent help you organize a
clean-up party for a local park.

STAND UP FOR WHAT YOU BELIEVE

Live wisely among those who are not believers,
and make the most of every opportunity.
Colossians 4:5 NLT

Sometimes I feel like I stick out like a sore thumb, Lord. I'm so different from the other kids. I'm surrounded by opposites—people who believe the opposite of me. Sometimes they're bigmouths! They shout what they believe in my ears and insist I agree with them. Ugh. Sometimes I want to put my fingers in my ears and hide under the table. These kids aren't easy to talk to, after all. Usually I just avoid them. Then I'm reminded that standing up for what I believe is a great way to share the gospel. You're always opening doors for conversations, Lord, so I step right through them. Help me to have the courage to go on speaking truth in love, even when it's hard. Amen.

. . . .

Be the Change
The next time you're at a restaurant,
treat your server with kindness.

A NEW WAY TO SEE THINGS!

*Do not be conformed to this world, but be transformed by the
renewal of your mind, that by testing you may discern what
is the will of God, what is good and acceptable and perfect.*
ROMANS 12:2 ESV

This is a cool verse, Lord, but I have a question: Do You *really*
mean that my mind can be made brand-new? Seriously?
Best. News. Ever! I'm tired of feeling stuck. Going along with
the crowd is getting old. But when I hang out with You, You give
me a whole new way of looking at things. You really do want to
make all things new in my life! I'm listening close because I don't
want to miss a thing. I want to know *Your* will, not the opinion
of the kid who sits next to me in science class. I want to do the
cool thing *You've* got planned for me to do, not the things other
kids want me to do. Thank You for making my heart and mind
new again, Lord. Amen.

. . . .

Be the Change
Make a list of five times God changed your mind.

ROOTED

And now, just as you accepted Christ Jesus as your Lord, you must continue to follow him. Let your roots grow down into him, and let your lives be built on him. Then your faith will grow strong in the truth you were taught, and you will overflow with thankfulness.
COLOSSIANS 2:6–7 NLT

I want to be like a tree with deep roots, Lord, so that I don't flip over sideways when strong winds blow. I've noticed that my faith gets stronger during the hard seasons, and I know it's because I'm leaning on You, not myself. This can only happen when my roots go *w-a-y* down deep into the ground—when I spend time reading my Bible and then praying about stuff. I try not to get nervous when I realize other kids are watching how I act. Maybe they're trying to figure out if I'm really a true Christian. They're checking out how I react when bad stuff happens. When my roots go deep, I set a better example for others. So today I choose to dig deep and to root myself in You. Amen.

. . . .

Be the Change
Take a book to a sick friend.

FIRM, BUT LOVING

Be on your guard; stand firm in the faith;
be courageous; be strong. Do everything in love.
1 CORINTHIANS 16:13–14 NIV

I've got the firm thing down, Lord. I know how to play the role of the tough guy. I've done it a lot. Sometimes I'm so firm I hurt other people's feelings. Oops. You want me to put my toughness in the mixer and mix it up with love. In fact, Your Word says I should do everything in love. Everything, Lord? Tough conversations with friends? Dealing with my kid sister? Talking to a teacher who's upset at me for not turning in my homework? Dealing with that girl who gives me such a tough time during PE? It's hard at times, but I'll give it my best shot because I know that others are watching. They see when I flip out. Help me, Father. May I always reflect You. Amen.

Be the Change
Ask a parent to help you deliver groceries to a sick neighbor.

NO SHAME HERE

For I am not ashamed of the gospel, for it is the
power of God for salvation to everyone who
believes, to the Jew first and also to the Greek.
ROMANS 1:16 ESV

Lord, I always tell people that I'm not ashamed of my faith, but I wonder if I'm being totally honest. There are times when I feel weird talking to others about Jesus and heaven and going to church. Some of them really don't get it. They treat me like I'm a weirdo. Things can get awkward, so I usually just clam up and don't mention it. I don't want to make people think I'm *too* different from the rest of the kids. Show me how to get over those nervous feelings, Lord. I want to share the gospel message with kids in school, in my neighborhood, and even when I'm playing sports. I want to make a difference in this world, Father, even when speaking the truth is hard. Amen.

. . . .

Be the Change
Donate your old toys and books that you no longer use.

ALL THE WORLD

*And he said to them, "Go into all the world and
proclaim the gospel to the whole creation."*
MARK 16:15 ESV

Confession time! I'm not the bravest kid in the world. Sometimes my knees start knocking when I try to talk to my best friend about my faith. I can't even imagine traveling across the world to talk to total strangers! I know that You can use me in any situation, so today I ask You to do just that, Lord. No matter where I am—at school, at play, at home, or on a trip with my family—You can speak through me to others. It doesn't have to be weird. Talking about You can happen in such a natural way that I don't even have to stress out about it. Every kid I come in contact with is one You died to save. When I remember that, talking with them about You is so much easier. Amen.

. . . .

Be the Change
*Ask a parent to help you host a blanket
drive for the homeless.*

BE WHO YOU SAY YOU ARE

Above all else, you must live in a way that brings honor to the good news about Christ. Then, whether I visit you or not, I will hear that all of you think alike. I will know that you are working together and are struggling side by side to get others to believe the good news.
PHILIPPIANS 1:27 CEV

Lord, I want to be the real deal. No phony-baloneys here! When people hang out with me at my house, I want them to see the same person they see at school. No faking it. I want to bring honor to Your name, in good times and in bad, in public and in private. I never want my faith to be a turnoff to those who are watching. Instead, I want them to look at me and say, "Wow! Now that's a kid I can really trust!" Help me to live in a way that brings honor to Your name, Lord. I want to be a true reflection of You, so others will get jump-up-and-down excited to learn more about You. Amen.

Be the Change
Instead of saying, "I'll be praying for you" when a friend is in need, stop and pray for that person—right then and there.

ALWAYS PREPARED

*But in your hearts honor Christ the Lord as holy,
always being prepared to make a defense to anyone
who asks you for a reason for the hope that is in
you; yet do it with gentleness and respect.*
1 PETER 3:15 ESV

It happens sometimes, Lord. I'm in the middle of a conversation with someone and say something about my faith. They roll their eyes and say something not-so-nice about Christianity—or about You. It really bugs me! I wish everyone would just agree with me. . . but of course they don't. You've given us free will, and many of the kids I know use it to stay as far away from Christianity as possible. They don't want anything to do with You. But I won't give up. I want to be ready—as this verse says—always prepared to make a defense for the hope that is in me. My testimony (my story of what You've done in my life) is the most powerful tool I've got, and I'm so excited to share it, no matter how the other kids respond. Thanks for the opportunity to shine Your light. Amen.

Be the Change
*Share the story of how you came to know
Jesus with your best friend.*

BE BOLD!

"But you will receive power when the Holy Spirit comes on you; and you will be my witnesses in Jerusalem, and in all Judea and Samaria, and to the ends of the earth."
ACTS 1:8 NIV

I feel like such a weakling at times, Lord, like I don't have an ounce of power inside of me. Then, just about the time I'm ready to pull the covers over my head, You rush in like a mighty wind and give me supernatural energy. Wow! The power that comes from Your Holy Spirit is different from anything I've ever experienced! I won't find it in an energy drink, or even through exercise or sports. Your heaven-sent power causes miracles to happen! It gives me courage to share my story with others. It also opens doors and gives me awesome opportunities to make a difference in this world. Thanks for this extra burst of boldness, Lord! Amen.

. . . .

Be the Change
Invite a friend over to watch Christian movies or read some Bible stories.

HiS NAME iS EXALTED

And you will say in that day: "Give thanks to the LORD,
call upon his name, make known his deeds among
the peoples, proclaim that his name is exalted."
ISAIAH 12:4 ESV

Lord, I don't always remember to exalt (lift up) Your name, but today I'm going to make up for that. I want to be a kid who really, truly loves You—with my words, my actions, and my prayers. So, I'll get right to it! You're an awesome, amazing God, and I love being Your kid. I have so much to be thankful for—an amazing family, good friends, food, a home to live in, clothes to wear. I know that all of that comes from You. Your Word says that You will take care of us, and You do. So, I praise You for all You've done. If anyone asks me why I'm so happy today, I'll tell them it's because You've blessed me so much. I praise You. Amen.

Be the Change
Place a "Jesus is the reason for the season!"
sign in your yard during the holidays.

LOVE. . .NO MATTER WHAT

But God shows his great love for us in this way:
Christ died for us while we were still sinners.
ROMANS 5:8 NCV

Lord, how is it possible that You can love me even when I totally mess things up? This "no matter what" kind of love amazes me. You even love those who don't love You back (something that must be really, really hard to do). You care for everyone, even those who don't appreciate it. You died on the cross for all people because You love them. If I tripped on the sidewalk and fell down, You would come rushing to my rescue, no matter how far You had to come. I'm never alone because You stick to me like glue. You have this same kind of love for all of mankind, people all over the world. You don't judge by skin color, by age, or by personality type. You're truly a "one love fits all" Father. I'm tickled pink about Your unconditional love! Amen.

. . . .

Be the Change
Extend friendship to someone who is your polar opposite.

LOVE GIVES

*"For God so loved the world, that he gave
his only Son, that whoever believes in him
should not perish but have eternal life."*
JOHN 3:16 ESV

I'll never understand how You did it, Father. . .how You sent Your only Son to earth to die for my sins. What an amazing sacrifice He made, dying on the cross for sinners like me. I've learned so much about giving from Your example. More than anything, I've discovered that love gives and gives and then gives some more. This is so different from how most of the kids I know live. Most of them just want what they want when they want it. But You've shown me that I need to be a giver if I want to make a difference in this world. And the truth is, I do want to make a difference. I know some people say I'm too young, but You use kids like me all the time to make people's lives happier. Show me how to give, Lord. Amen.

. . . .

Be the Change
*Have a parent help you prepare a meal or
bake a dessert for an elderly neighbor.*

GIVE UP YOUR OWN WAY

*Then [Jesus] said to the crowd, "If any of you wants
to be my follower, you must give up your own way,
take up your cross daily, and follow me. If you try
to hang on to your life, you will lose it. But if you
give up your life for my sake, you will save it."*
LUKE 9:23–24 NLT

Can I be honest about something, Lord? I'm not really a big fan of the words "give up your own way." If I'm being honest, I like to have my own way, thank You very much. But You're flip-flopping my thinking. It's not "my way or the highway" anymore. It's Your way, Father, because You want me to think of others first. Other kids are watching how I live, and I want them to know I care. This might take some work on my part. It won't come naturally to give up my own way. It hurts a little just thinking about it. But I'm in this for the long haul, Lord. Keep changing my heart and my thoughts, so that I will see people through Your eyes and want what's best for them, not just what's best for me. Amen.

Be the Change
*Offer to take out the trash or do another chore you
usually don't like, and complete it with a smile.*

WISH THEM WELL

*Wish good for those who harm you; wish them well
and do not curse them. Be happy with those who
are happy, and be sad with those who are sad.*
ROMANS 12:14–15 NCV

Oh, I get so mad at people sometimes, Lord! I just want to get even when they hurt me. It seems fair to get back at them. But You don't think like that. If I want people in my world to change—to be more like You—then *I* need an attitude adjustment. Instead of getting mad when people hurt me, I need to follow the advice in this scripture and pray that good things will happen to them. It's not easy to wish them well, especially when I'm still mad at them, but I want my heart to be like Yours. So change my stinking thinking, Father. I want to speak blessing, not cursing, over my friends. Make me a giver, not a taker. I want to be known as a kid who truly cares about others, even those who've done me wrong. Help me, I pray. Amen.

. . . .

Be the Change
*Send a card or letter of encouragement to
someone who has hurt your feelings.*

JOINED TOGETHER

I beg you, brothers and sisters, by the name of our Lord Jesus Christ that all of you agree with each other and not be split into groups. I beg that you be completely joined together by having the same kind of thinking and the same purpose.
1 CORINTHIANS 1:10 NCV

This is a hard one, Lord. I'm used to hanging out with people who agree with me. I usually just keep my distance from the ones who disagree. Life is easier this way. But You didn't call me to an easy life, did You? After all, it's hard to be "joined together" with people I'm not even trying to get along with. Could You do me a little favor, Lord? Soften my heart. Make it squishy in Your hands, especially when I'm around people who don't love You. Help me to love, despite our differences. And while You're at it, please soften their hearts too. I want to live at peace with everyone—at school and in my neighborhood—bringing joy to Your heart as we walk in unity. Amen.

· ·

Be the Change
Offer to help your mom clean the kitchen.

LED BY LOVE

Let love be your guide. Christ loved us and offered his life for us as a sacrifice that pleases God.
EPHESIANS 5:2 CEV

If my family and I went for a long walk in the wilderness we would definitely take a cell phone so we could have GPS. It would be really scary without it. We wouldn't know which way to go. Love is like a GPS app. It can guide me through rough stuff. I would get totally lost without it. Love leads the way like nothing else can. It clears a path better than any weed eater. It cuts through weeds, protects me from tripping and injuring my knee, and shines a light on the path so that I know which way to go. This is especially helpful when nighttime comes and the trail is dark. More than anything, love helps me connect with the other kids around me (the kids who are like me, and the kids who are different). Show me how to love as You love, Lord. Amen.

Be the Change
Offer to weed your neighbor's garden.

WHILE WE WERE YET SINNERS

*But God shows his love for us in that while we
were still sinners, Christ died for us.*
ROMANS 5:8 ESV

You didn't wait until I had my act together to whisper, "I love you" in my ear, did You, Lord? Nope. You said, "I love you, kid," while I was still figuring things out. Some of my friends and family members are still a little lost, Lord. They're not interested in hearing about You. Most of them seem okay with how they are. They don't want to change one little bit. I haven't figured out how to reach out to them. I want to share with them my love for You, but I don't want to push them away. Show me how to follow Your example, Lord—how to show the kind of love that leads to understanding and change. I need Your help with this one, Father. Amen.

. . . .

Be the Change
*Leave a kind note or drawing (on a separate piece
of paper!) inside your favorite library book.*

PAID IN FULL

Let no debt remain outstanding, except the
continuing debt to love one another, for
whoever loves others has fulfilled the law.
ROMANS 13:8 NIV

Father, I don't like to owe people stuff. It's an icky feeling to know that you can't pay something back. That's why I love what Jesus did for me on the cross. He took my debt and paid it in full. He said, "No charge, kid! I've got this one!" Now all He asks of me is to love Him and love others. That might sound easy, but to be honest there are some people who are hard to love. You know who they are, Lord. They get on my nerves. They bug me. They sneak in my room and play with my stuff. They can be a real pain. But You say to love them anyway, so that's what I'm going to do. I don't want to owe anyone a love debt! Amen.

. . . .

Be the Change
Send a card to a loved one today.

A FUZZY BLANKET OF LOVE

Above all, keep loving one another earnestly,
since love covers a multitude of sins.
1 PETER 4:8 ESV

Oh boy, have I messed up a lot of stuff, Lord. I've said the wrong things, done the wrong things, made the wrong decisions. Ouch! I get it wrong a lot. But every time You cover my mess-ups with Your great blanket of love. It covers all my sins (and insults, and bitterness, and pain). Show me how to use this blanket to fix broken friendships, I pray. I want everything to be good—between my friends, my family members, the kids at school, and even my teachers. Your Word says that love is the greatest gift of all, so today I offer it to those I've hurt, so that we can be friends again. I'm really going to need Your help with this one! Amen.

. . . .

Be the Change
Show Christ's love to someone who has
treated you in an unloving way.

THE PEACE OF CHRIST

*Let the peace of Christ, to which you were indeed called
in one body, rule in your hearts; and be thankful.*
COLOSSIANS 3:15 NASB

I love this verse, Lord! It's Your peace I want. Nothing else will do. When I allow Your peace to rule my heart, I'm completely content. I don't question every little thing. I'm not uneasy all the time or wondering if I made the right decisions. I'm truly resting in You because I know You have my best interest at heart. This same peace helps me get along with others and avoid fighting, even when we don't always share the same opinions or beliefs. Your peace covers it all. Wow, that's pretty amazing, if I stop to think about it. What a great peacemaker You are, Lord! Amen.

. . . .

Be the Change
*Ask your mom or dad to drive an elderly neighbor
to the grocery store or doctor's office.*

LIGHT-BRIGHT!

You used to be like people living in the dark, but now you are people of the light because you belong to the Lord. So act like people of the light and make your light shine. Be good and honest and truthful, as you try to please the Lord.
EPHESIANS 5:8–10 CEV

Lord, sometimes this world feels kind of dark and creepy. I try to shine my light, but I wonder if I'm making any difference at all. The kids around me are doing things they shouldn't. Ugh! It really bugs me! I'm embarrassed and ashamed at the things they say and do, but they don't seem to care that they're breaking Your heart. That's why I'm so grateful for this reminder in Your Word that I belong to You, that it's really *Your* light I'm shining. Whew! It's not all on me. What a relief! I can take a breather and relax because You're the one doing the work. I'm just Your helper. As I step out into this great big world, give me creative ideas so that I can shine in a way that others will be drawn to You. I praise You for the joy of making a change, Lord. Amen.

. . . .

Be the Change

Here's a fun idea: draw pictures of flowers and have a parent take you to a nursing home to give them to the residents.

i CAN'T WAIT TO BLESS OTHERS!

Do not let kindness and truth leave you; bind them around your neck, write them on the tablet of your heart.
PROVERBS 3:3 NASB

God, I get it now! The very best way to bless others is to make kindness and truth an everyday part of my life. When my heart is softened toward others, when I genuinely care about their needs, I'll want to bring hope to the hopeless, love to those feeling unloved. I can't wait to bless them. Oh, what a fun and adventurous life this is—loving others as You love them. I'm filled with so many ideas, dreaming up so many different ways I can bring hope. When others see me, I want them to say, "Wow! That one's really got a heart for others!" With Your help, I will be that sort of person, Lord. Amen.

. . . .

Be the Change

Collect blankets for a women's shelter or for the homeless.

SERVE ONE ANOTHER

*As each has received a gift, use it to serve one
another, as good stewards of God's varied grace.*
1 PETER 4:10 ESV

I like to be the boss, Lord. Just put me in charge and I'll do my best work, especially if others are watching. Look at me shine! Everyone will be glad they picked me to be the leader. I'll show them I've got the goods! But You're teaching me that it's best to humble myself and take on the role of servant at times, to care about the desires of others, to make sure their needs are met. Today I choose to change my world by paying attention to what's going on in the lives of those around me. When I'm paying attention, I know how to pray. And maybe, just maybe, You might show me how to meet some of their needs without being the top guy on the totem pole. Amen.

. . . .

Be the Change
Send cards to soldiers serving overseas.

OVERFLOWING WITH HOPE

*May the God of hope fill you with all joy and peace
as you trust in him, so that you may overflow
with hope by the power of the Holy Spirit.*
ROMANS 15:13 NIV

I know what the word "overflowing" looks like, Lord. I've seen it happen: in the bathtub, the kitchen sink, even the dishwasher. I even saw an overflow during a rainstorm once. The streets filled with water, to the top of the curb! I guess some people think "overflow" means "too much." But when it comes to giving love and hope to others, I don't think it's possible to go overboard. You want me to overflow with hope in every situation, to completely trust in You, even when things seem impossible. When I spill over the top with hope, others will see and want to put their hope in You too, Lord. So, fill me to the tippy-top, and then let it overflow! Amen.

. . . .

Be the Change
Give a hug to someone you care about.

HOPE BRINGS PEACE

Jesus said to them again, "Peace be with you.
As the Father has sent me, even so I am sending you."
JOHN 20:21 ESV

It makes sense, Lord. When my hope is high, my peace rises too. I'm not fretting and worrying about what tomorrow might bring, so I'm calm, cool, and collected, even on the day of the big test! That's what happens when I trust in You. I want to share that hope so that others can be peaceful too. So many of the people I know—friends at school, neighbors, family members—seem hopeless. You sent Your Son to bring hope to the world, and now You're sending me to do the same. I can't believe You trust me with this. I'm just a kid! What an honor to be chosen by You, Lord. May all people come to fully know the hope that only You can bring. Amen.

. . . .

Be the Change
Adopt a grandparent. Treat this person as your own,
with all the affection a grandparent deserves!

WELCOME TO THE NEIGHBORHOOD!

And so, Lord, where do I put my hope? My only hope is in you.
PSALM 39:7 NLT

Here's a fun idea, Lord! I can be a welcome committee to new people moving into my neighborhood. Give me creative ideas so that I can make my new neighbors feel right at home as soon as they move in. I bet it can feel kind of weird being new in town. You don't know where you fit or if people will accept you. That's why it's so cool to have people say, "Hey, welcome to the neighborhood! We're glad you're here!" That always does the trick. I'm learning how to welcome others from You, Lord. You welcomed me into Your neighborhood with open arms, after all. You brought me into Your family and loved me so much that I felt right at home. I want to learn from Your example, Lord. Amen.

. . . .

Be the Change
Ask a parent to help you start a "Welcome Wagon" committee in your neighborhood.

TREE OF LIFE

Hope deferred makes the heart sick,
but a dream fulfilled is a tree of life.
PROVERBS 13:12 NLT

I love the image of a "tree of life," Lord. That's what I want to be, to all the kids I hang out with and play with, or to the friend sitting next to me in class. I want my branches to spread out super-duper wide, to offer friendship, especially to the kids who don't seem to have many friends. Some of the kids I know are going through stuff, *really* tough stuff. Some of them are embarrassed to let others know. Show me how to help them through the not-so-great times. I want to make a difference in this world, no matter who I'm with—young or old. I want to bring hope and life to everyone I know, Lord. Please help me. Amen.

. . . .

Be the Change
Help your parents plan a neighborhood
cookout. Invite everyone on your block for
an afternoon of fun and great food.

HiS NAME BRINGS HOPE

"And his name will be the hope of all the world."
MATTHEW 12:21 NLT

Lord, there's so much power in Your name! When I speak the name of Jesus, demons have to run in fear! Wow! That's better than a scene from a movie! Mountains are zapped! Prayers get answered. Lives are changed, not just here but for eternity. The name of Jesus brings hope, not just to the icky stuff I'm going through, not just to those I love, but to people around the world, even kids I've never met. That's why the enemy is trying so hard to get rid of the name of Jesus, because he knows there's power in that name. But I'll go on shouting, "Praise You, Jesus!" at the top of my lungs and watch as miracles take place. What an awesome, holy name, Lord! Amen.

. . . .

Be the Change
*Invite friends over to make and send care
packages to men and woman in the military.*

THE SOURCE OF HOPE

I pray that God, the source of hope, will fill you completely with joy and peace because you trust in him. Then you will overflow with confident hope through the power of the Holy Spirit.
ROMANS 15:13 NLT

Tap, tap, tap! It's me, knocking on the door, Lord! I'm looking for hope. I'm glad I finally came to Your door instead of the ones I usually try. Talk about going to the wrong address! I've been looking in the wrong places. I usually tap on the doors of my friends, my family, or even my coaches or teachers, hoping they will give me hope. But You've been teaching me an important lesson. I'll always come up empty unless I tap into You, the true source of hope. Oh, those other things will lift my spirits for a little while, but if I want long-term hope, I need to stay plugged in to You because You're the one who created hope in the first place. You completely fill me, top to bottom, with a lasting hope, one that doesn't play peek-a-boo when I'm having a hard day. Thanks for giving me hope! Amen.

. . . .

Be the Change
Bring hope to your teacher at school by offering to help her set up her classroom.

AN AWESOME INVITATION

This hope is a strong and trustworthy anchor for our souls.
It leads us through the curtain into God's inner sanctuary.
HEBREWS 6:19 NLT

Thanks for sending me a personal invitation to spend time with You in Your holy place, Lord. Talk about exciting! It's better than getting an invitation from a movie star or famous singer. When I say yes to Your invitation, I get so excited because I know cool stuff will happen when I hang out with You. It's also a great place to talk about all of the hard stuff I've been going through! You open Your arms and say, "Tell Me your troubles. Rest awhile in Me." When I take the time to do that, miraculous things happen. My hope is restored. I'm jazzed up with energy from the inside out. And I'm ready to make a difference in my world once again. Thanks for the cool invitation, Father. I love hanging out with You! Amen.

. . . .

Be the Change
Spend quality time with a friend or loved one today.

THE GOLDEN RULE

*"Do to others as you would
have them do to you."*
LUKE 6:31 NIV

To be honest, Lord, sometimes I want to say, "Do unto others" and leave off the "as you would have them do to you" part. Is it awful to admit that I usually put myself first? I know, I know! Your Word says I should think of others first if I want to be a world changer, so I'll try harder. I'll give it my best. I'll treat others according to the Golden Rule—as I would want to be treated myself. If I truly live that way, people will want what I've got—a relationship with You. It's a win-win situation when I follow Your lead, but You and I both know I can't do this on my own. That's why I need You so much! Thanks for helping me, Lord. Amen.

Be the Change
Offer to help a friend with chores.

OTHERS BEFORE SELF

*Now make me completely happy! Live in harmony
by showing love for each other. Be united in what
you think, as if you were only one person.*
PHILIPPIANS 2:2 CEV

Others before self. Not how I usually live, Lord. It's me, myself, and I most of the time. I want what I want when I want it. Hungry? I open the refrigerator. Cold? I get a coat or blanket. If my shoes are pinching my toes, I ask my parents for a new pair. Problem solved! But I get it, Lord. You want me to look after others, not just myself. That homeless man who's shivering in the cold? I can give him a blanket. That woman in the shelter who's hungry? I can help feed her. That child without shoes? I can donate mine that I've outgrown. There are so many things I can do to put others ahead of myself. Give me creative ideas, I pray. Amen.

. . . .

Be the Change
*Ask your parent to help you make a food
donation to the local food bank.*

LOVE ONE ANOTHER

*Beloved, if God so loved us,
we also ought to love one another.*
1 JOHN 4:11 ESV

This is such a simple command: love one another. And I do my best, Lord, though some people are a *l-o-t* harder to love than others. I don't know how You love the people who have done terrible things, but the Bible says You do. The man behind bars for that horrible crime? You died for him. That woman who is really mean to her little girl? You still love her, no matter how she acts. I don't really get it, but I want to try. Show me how to love others, "in spite of." Then give me ideas for how to show that love—whether it's to the kids sitting next to me at the lunch table or people who are different from me. I'm excited to learn, Lord. Amen.

. . . .

Be the Change
Volunteer at a homeless shelter.

THINK OF OTHERS AS BETTER

Don't be selfish; don't try to impress others.
Be humble, thinking of others as better than yourselves.
PHILIPPIANS 2:3 NLT

Oh boy. I might be in trouble with this one. I sometimes show off. I try to impress others. But Your Word tells me that I have to think of others as better than myself. I get it, Lord. Everyone wants to feel special, after all. That kid who sits next to me in math class—the one everyone picks on? I can make her feel included. That coach who lost his job and wonders if he'll ever be able to provide for his family? I can pray for him and maybe even ask members of my church to donate money to buy Christmas gifts for his kids. That boy who's always in trouble at school? I can let him know that he's important to You. You're giving me all sorts of ideas for how I can make others feel special. When I'm focused on "them," then "me" isn't at the front of my mind. It's an awesome way to live, Lord. Amen.

. . . .

Be the Change
Create goody bags for people in a retirement home.

PAUSE TO LOOK

"But a Samaritan, as he traveled, came where the man was; and when he saw him, he took pity on him."
LUKE 10:33 NIV

I love this story of the Good Samaritan, Lord. My favorite part of the story? The Good Samaritan stopped to check out the situation instead of crossing to the other side of the street like the other guys. They didn't want to see. I think it's because they knew they would have to do something. But this guy? Check him out! He decided to look closer. He stopped, looked, and listened . . .then acted. I can't lie, sometimes I walk right by people in need. It's true! I see kids in school who are in need of friendship, love, and forgiveness, and I ignore them. I'm not trying to be mean. I'm just distracted by my own stuff. But no more. I want to be a giver, Lord, someone who pays attention. So, open my eyes wider than ever to see those in need around me. Give me Your vision, I pray. Amen.

. . . .

Be the Change
*Ask your parents if you can "adopt" a missionary.
Let others know about this person's great work.*

iT MATTERS TO GOD

*The LORD tests the righteous, but his soul hates
the wicked and the one who loves violence.*
PSALM 11:5 ESV

Sometimes I get a little nervous that You're watching my every move, Lord. It's especially embarrassing when I mess up or when I treat others badly. You care a lot about how I treat my brothers and sisters, the kids I hang out with, and the boy who sits next to me in school. You're also watching how I treat the kids that no one else seems to notice—the girl in the wheelchair, the boy in special ed, the kid who has to take medicine because he's always sick. You care about each one. It makes You smile when I take the time to care for those who are less fortunate than I am, because You want me to make a difference and show everyone that they matter. Thanks for that reminder, Lord. Amen.

. . . .

Be the Change
Read to patients at a nursing home.

OTHERS BEFORE SELF

Finally, all of you, be like-minded, be sympathetic, love one another, be compassionate and humble.
1 PETER 3:8 NIV

All of you. Wow, I get it, Lord. There was a time when I thought only a few people were called by You to care for the needy, the poor, the homeless, the widows, and so on. For sure, I didn't think You were talking about me! Missionaries, pastors, church leaders. . . Aren't these the ones You want to take care of the sick and homeless? Are You really asking *me* to get involved too? I'm not very old, but I'm willing to give it a try. I guess I'm part of the "all of you" group, and it's my job to make a difference in the lives of people in need too. Show me how to link arms with grown-ups so that I can be useful. Use me in ways You've never used me before. I give myself to Your service, Father. Amen.

. . . .

Be the Change
Offer to help (send out a newsletter, raise funds, host a drive for) a local or foreign missions' organization.

OUTDO ONE ANOTHER

Love one another with brotherly affection.
Outdo one another in showing honor.
ROMANS 12:10 ESV

This is a fun idea, Lord! You want us to outdo one another, not with our talents or treasures, but in showing honor to one another. I love a good competition, but sometimes I'm in it to win it, if You know what I mean. It's all about me. It'll be fun to try this new way, putting others first. Show me some ideas, okay? Maybe I could open doors for people. Offer a smile or a hand to help a young mom with a crying toddler. Helping an elderly person with her walker might be another fun idea. There are so many little ways I can make a difference in someone's day. My imagination is going crazy just thinking about it! I can't wait to get started. Give me creative ideas, I pray. Amen.

. . . .

Be the Change
Ask a parent to help you take a meal to a single parent.

PURIFIED BY YOU

*Having purified your souls by your obedience
to the truth for a sincere brotherly love, love
one another earnestly from a pure heart.*
1 PETER 1:22 ESV

I'm just learning what it means to be purified, Lord. When gold is put in the fire, the icky part falls off. Only the good stuff remains. (I would love to watch that!) It's not always easy to be purified, but I want to give it my best shot so I can be the best me I can be. Out with the bad stuff, in with the good! I'll only make a difference in the lives of others if they actually want to be around me. I get that now. I guess I'll have to be purified if I want to be a true and lasting friend. Show me how to really, truly love others, no matter who they are or what they've done. Purify my heart, I pray. May all of the icky stuff fall off and only what's holy remain. Amen.

. . . .

Be the Change
Ask your pastor to help you host a food drive for the needy.

EACH PART WORKING PROPERLY

He makes the whole body fit together perfectly. As each part does its own special work, it helps the other parts grow, so that the whole body is healthy and growing and full of love.
EPHESIANS 4:16 NLT

Lord, sometimes when I hang out with my friends, things go wrong. People get their feelings hurt. We end up in a fight or argument. Ugh! What a mess! The whole thing gets kind of weird and nobody really knows how to fix it. I know You want me to be at peace with others, and that means I have to figure out how to fix it when things go wrong. So, today I'm going to pray for those in my group instead of complaining about them. I pray for peace, of course, but I also pray that each friend would learn to love You and each other. If that happens, we'll make a strong team, ready to take on the world. Help my friends, I pray. Amen.

- -

Be the Change
Be willing to be a part of the group, not the leader.

PEER PRESSURE

Don't take part in doing those worthless things that are done in the dark. Instead, show how wrong they are. It is disgusting even to talk about what is done in the dark.
EPHESIANS 5:11–12 CEV

Peer pressure. Following the crowd. Why do I keep getting caught in this trap, Lord? One minute I'm absolutely positively sure *no one* can talk me into doing something bad; the next minute I'm following the crowd, doing the wrong thing. This happens a lot when my friends are gossiping about others or cutting people down behind their backs. I don't mean to do it. Somehow, I get sucked in. I'm always so ashamed afterward. I vow to do better next time. Ugh! Why do I keep slipping up? This time I really mean it. I need Your help, Lord. Whenever my friends start up with the usual gossip, give me the courage to back away. I don't want to go along with the crowd anymore, Lord. Amen.

Be the Change
Send a card to someone who's hurting.

NO BULLYING!

Whoever walks with the wise becomes wise,
but the companion of fools will suffer harm.
PROVERBS 13:20 ESV

Bullies drive me crazy, Lord! Doesn't matter if they're kids on the playground picking on me or if they're friends of my mom, trying to hurt her with their words. You know what it feels like to be hurt by the words of others, Lord. Your Son went through every emotion when He came to earth. He decided to go on loving the bullies, even when they hung him on a cross. I'll never know how He did that! And He even forgave them. He looked down from the cross and said, "Father, forgive them, for they know not what they do" (Luke 23:34 ESV). I definitely need to learn from His example. I want to help put a stop to bullying. I won't join in from now on. And help me protect those who are being bullied, I pray. I want to make a difference, Lord. Amen.

. . . .

Be the Change
Include those who are rarely included.

PREJUDICE

Do not conform to the pattern of this world, but be transformed by the renewing of your mind. Then you will be able to test and approve what God's will is—his good, pleasing and perfect will.
ROMANS 12:2 NIV

They look different, Lord. They don't fit in. They speak a different language or dress a different way. Their skin color is different. They're from a different culture, one I'm not familiar with. Some of them are trying to figure out where they fit in at school. The kids in my group haven't been very helpful. In fact, they whisper and talk about these people behind their backs, sometimes saying really mean things. Today, please show me how I can do away with prejudice, the belief that one person is better than another. I want to include everyone—in my neighborhood, my church, and my school. When You look at Your kids, You don't see people divided by languages and cultures. You see one big happy family. Show me how I can help other kids feel like they fit in, I pray. Amen.

. . . .

Be the Change
Ask your friend about his or her culture.

THE REAL DEAL

If anyone says, "I love God," and hates his brother, he is a liar; for he who does not love his brother whom he has seen cannot love God whom he has not seen.

1 JOHN 4:20 ESV

I have to confess, I'm not always who I pretend to be, Lord. Sometimes I'm sweet to people to their face but say rude things about them when they look away. Sure, I put up with them when we're together, but I don't really love them the way I pretend to. I fake it because I want to look godly when others are watching. (I feel icky even confessing that!) But when I turn the other way, the real me comes out. Oops. You don't like this kind of hypocrisy. I know that, Lord. So, please help me. I want to be the same kid when I turn away from a conversation as I was when chatting face-to-face. If I really love someone, I'll be a "real deal" friend. You take this very seriously, I know, so help me. Amen.

Be the Change
Send an encouraging message to someone who's been feeling like they don't have any friends.

DON'T TRIP THEM UP

So let's stop condemning each other. Decide instead to live in such a way that you will not cause another believer to stumble and fall.
ROMANS 14:13 NLT

This is a tough one, Lord! Sometimes I can be pretty critical. When someone else makes a mistake, I point it out. I sure know how to bring a frown to my friends' faces sometimes. Why do I feel like I have to point out people's mess-ups, anyway? Most of them are really trying hard to do the right thing. And it's not like I never mess up. I do! It's embarrassing when people point out my mistakes. I'm so sorry I treat people like this, Father. I long to be an encourager, not a discourager. When I get to heaven, I don't want to see a long line of people who say, "I remember her. She used to tell me I was wrong all the time." Instead, I want to see a line of people who all remember what a great friend and encourager I was. Help me with this, I pray. Amen.

Be the Change
Offer to color in a coloring book with a younger kid.

BE A GOD-PLEASER

*For am I now seeking the approval of man, or of God?
Or am I trying to please man? If I were still trying to
please man, I would not be a servant of Christ.*
GALATIANS 1:10 ESV

I want to please You, Lord, but (I confess) there are times I'm more interested in pleasing the kids around me. I say yes to things I should say no to because I want the popular kids to like me. I try extra hard to fit in because being part of their group feels good, at least for a while. Sometimes I work too hard at this. And that's not all. Sometimes I get really busy, hanging out at my friend's house or going to the mall. This isn't always Your will, Father. Sometimes You want me to back away, to say no, to spend more time away from the crowd and with You instead. I get it. You always accept me. I don't have to impress You. From now on, I will try to please You and not worry so much about the people around me. Amen.

. . . .

Be the Change
Do a good deed. . .in secret.

DON'T GIVE IN

My son, if sinful men entice you, do not give in to them.
PROVERBS 1:10 NIV

Temptation is hard, Lord! There are times I fight temptation with everything in me! Then there are other times when I don't even try. I tumble headfirst into sin without giving it any worry at all. Shame on me! I don't want to be one who gives in easily. I want to go down kicking and screaming when temptation comes my way. Please don't let me get into friendships that pull me away from You. There are people out there who want me to mess up, but that's not what I want. I want to impact my world, and that means I sometimes end up hanging out with people who don't know You yet, but I don't ever want to compromise my faith or give up on what I know to be true. Guard my heart and my spirit, I pray. Amen.

. . . .

Be the Change
Offer to pray for someone who is hurting.

DON'T BE FOOLED

Don't fool yourselves. Bad friends will destroy you.
1 Corinthians 15:33 CEV

It's a trap, Lord! I get fooled by people who seem good, but they're really not. I fall right into the trap and hang out with them. Next thing you know, they're trying to get me to do things I shouldn't, like lying, cheating on tests, or being really unkind to others. Once I'm caught in the trap, it's hard to get out. I want to be a good example, but when I'm stuck in the trap, it's so hard! This isn't how You want me to live, Father! I'm supposed to be a leader, not a follower. I don't want to go backward. . .ever. No more traps for me! And while You're at it, set my friends free from the traps they're in too. I want to bring as many to heaven with me as I can. Thanks for helping me, Lord. Amen.

Be the Change
Ask a teacher to help you host an after-school program at a local elementary school.

HELD

*"So do not fear, for I am with you; do not be dismayed,
for I am your God. I will strengthen you and help you;
I will uphold you with my righteous right hand."*
ISAIAH 41:10 NIV

Sometimes I feel really close to You, Lord. It's weird, but it's almost like I'm curled up next to You, like You're holding me in Your lap. I love that feeling. If You weren't there, everything would be a big mess. All of my mistakes would seem bigger. I would probably feel like giving up. But You promise never to leave me. You'll go on holding me as long as it takes to get through my problem. You love me that much. Wow! You've done so much in my life, and that gets me really excited. I'm always telling other people how You got our family through the tough times, like when my dad lost his job and You got him another one. Or when my grandma got sick and we prayed, then she got better. I know You'll do the same thing for others too. Thanks for holding us all so close. What a good and loving Father You are! Amen.

. . . .

Be the Change

Write down your testimony and share it with someone who loves you. Let others know what God has done in Your life.

i want it. . .now!

"For what will it profit a man if he gains the whole world and forfeits his soul? Or what shall a man give in return for his soul?"
MATTHEW 16:26 ESV

Sometimes I feel like that little girl in the movie *Willy Wonka and the Chocolate Factory*, Lord. I find myself saying, "I want it, and I want it *now!*" Then I'm reminded that getting what I wish for isn't always for the best. What good would it do me to receive all that I ever longed for, only to lose my soul? Nothing is worth that! You're teaching me that life isn't about stuff. It's about loving You and being loved in return. It's about losing my life, giving up my selfishness, so that I can find it in You. It's about sharing the joy of my journey with others—kids at school, neighbors, and so on. I don't ever want to swap out any of that for temporary happiness, Lord. It's not worth it, and I'm glad I've figured that out. Amen.

. . . .

Be the Change
That very thing you've been wishing for? Save up your allowance to buy it and give to a friend.

PERFECT HARMONY

Above all, clothe yourselves with love, which binds us all together in perfect harmony. And let the peace that comes from Christ rule in your hearts. For as members of one body you are called to live in peace. And always be thankful.
COLOSSIANS 3:14–15 NLT

Lord, this is a big, wide world, filled with all sorts of people of every race and creed. When I think about all of us living together in harmony, it feels impossible. Lots of people don't believe in You and don't think I should, either. Wow! They can't ever make me stop believing Lord, I promise. But I'm still supposed to be kind to these people, even though we're total opposites. Please help me! I want to live at peace with others. This will only happen if I treat people with love. Maybe, if I love my way through, I'll change a few minds along the way. That's my prayer, anyway! Amen!

. . . .

Be the Change
Invite a new friend over for dinner.

GOOD MEASURE

*"Give, and it will be given to you. Good measure,
pressed down, shaken together, running over,
will be put into your lap. For with the measure
you use it will be measured back to you."*
LUKE 6:38 ESV

I remember going to the deli with my mom, Lord, and watching the butcher put the meat on the scale. Even though it weighed more than what mom asked for, he wrapped it up anyway and didn't charge her for the extra. That's how it is when I serve You. You're always giving me more than I expect. You're a generous God! And I see now that You want me to have that same generous spirit. When I give (even when I don't have much to give), You give back in good measure (like the butcher!). Pressed down, shaken together, running over! That's how You weigh things, Father. You give and give and give! Have I mentioned how grateful I am for Your generosity? Praise You, Lord. Amen.

Be the Change
Surprise your mom with breakfast in bed.

CARING FOR THE DISABLED

*If anyone is poor among your fellow Israelites in any of
the towns of the land the L*ord *your God is giving you,
do not be hardhearted or tightfisted toward them. Rather,
be openhanded and freely lend them whatever they need.*
Deuteronomy 15:7–8 niv

Lord, I want to do a better job of reaching out to the disabled in my community. There are times when I feel totally stuck. I don't know what to do. So I do nothing. I stand off to the side and let other people take over. But now You're giving me creative ideas! I can volunteer in a special needs' classroom at church. I can play with a friend who's in a wheelchair. I can help my mom make a meal for a caregiver. I can offer to clean the home of a person who's hospitalized so that it's ready when she returns home. I want to be helpful, Lord. Please give me Your heart and Your attitude toward everyone, I pray. Amen.

. . . .

Be the Change
Help a caregiver out with a special meal or dessert.

CARING. . .MORE AND MORE

This is my prayer for you: that your love will grow
more and more; that you will have knowledge
and understanding with your love.
PHILIPPIANS 1:9 NCV

Sometimes I look at the people in my life—my parents, grand-parents, siblings, aunts, uncles, cousins, friends—and I think, "I couldn't possibly love them any more than I do right now!" My love runs deep, Lord. But You're showing me that I can always grow my love (like a plant grows in a garden). I can love in actions, (doing kind things) and with my words (speaking kind things). My love for You can grow too! When I spend more time with You, I feel closer and closer to You. It's such a special feeling to know You love me too! You've been loving me all along, even before I was born. That's crazy to think about! Wow, I love this kind of love, Lord! Amen.

. . . .

Be the Change
Tell family members how much you love them.

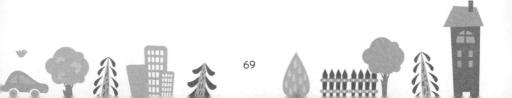

69

CARING FOR SHUT-INS

Bear one another's burdens, and so fulfill the law of Christ.
GALATIANS 6:2 ESV

They aren't able to take care of themselves, Lord. They depend on others for everything—their food, clothing, medicine, and so on. I can't imagine what that must feel like. These sweet older people hardly ever get to leave their homes because they're too weak. They must be so lonely. Show me how I can help. Should I visit? Read to them from their favorite book? Sing songs together? Offer to clean up or help cook meals? Maybe I could sweep the driveway or tidy up the kitchen. There's got to be something I can do to help make their days sweeter. Show me, I pray. Amen.

. . . .

Be the Change

With a parent's permission or supervision, play board games with a neighbor who can't leave the house often.

CARING FOR THE GRIEVING

*"He will wipe away every tear from their eyes,
and there will be no more death, sadness, crying,
or pain, because all the old ways are gone."*
REVELATION 21:4 NCV

I don't know how to help my friend, Lord. Someone she loved very much has passed away. She's so sad, and I don't blame her! It makes me sad too! I wish I knew how to take her pain away. I speak kind words, but that's not enough. Show me how to be a comfort to her, Lord. Can I send her a card? Bake her favorite cookies? Listen to her talk about her loved one? Should I offer to clean her house when people are coming over, or maybe take care of her dog during the funeral? I'll do my best to be there for her. When I give her tight hugs, I hope she feels Your presence. More than anything, I want this amazing friend to know she is not alone, she's not forgotten. Help me as I reach out to her during this tough time, I pray. Amen.

. . . .

Be the Change
*Ask a parent to help you set up a meal train
for a family who's lost a loved one.*

CARING FOR THE SICK

Is anyone among you suffering? Let him pray. Is anyone cheerful? Let him sing praise. Is anyone among you sick? Let him call for the elders of the church, and let them pray over him, anointing him with oil in the name of the Lord. And the prayer of faith will save the one who is sick, and the Lord will raise him up. And if he has committed sins, he will be forgiven.

JAMES 5:13–15 ESV

When people are sick, I never know what to do. Mostly, my mom says I have to stay away from them if they're contagious. I know I can pray, of course (and I do), but what else can I do to cheer up a sick friend? Can I send her a message? Make a really big card and get all of her friends to sign it? Should I make a "Get Well Soon!" banner and give it to her mom to hang in her room? Can I call her on the phone and tell her that I'm praying? Give me creative ideas to lift her spirits, I pray. Amen.

Be the Change
*Make the world's largest "Get Well Soon!"
card and have everyone in class sign it!*

CARING FOR THOSE IN NEED AS YOU CARE FOR YOURSELF

" 'Love the Lord your God with all your heart and with all your soul and with all your mind.' This is the first and greatest commandment. And the second is like it: 'Love your neighbor as yourself.' "
MATTHEW 22:37–39 NIV

Last time I got sick, I got the royal treatment, Lord! My mom drove me to the doctor's office and picked up my medicine at the pharmacy. When we got home, she brought me hot soup and crackers. She took my temperature every hour and made sure I took all of my medicine (even the icky-tasting stuff). No matter how bad I felt, she was right there to tell me I would be better soon. I really needed that! Mom cares so much about me. That's the way You want me to be with others—not just when they're sick, but all of the time. You want me to show the same tender loving care and treat them as I would want to be treated. I'll do my best, Lord. Amen.

. . . .

Be the Change
Next time one of your family members is sick, find a way that you can be helpful to them.

CHURCH FRIENDS

So then, as we have opportunity, let us do good to everyone,
and especially to those who are of the household of faith.
GALATIANS 6:10 ESV

People at my church are like my family, Lord. I've got brothers and sisters by the hundreds. (That's cool to think about!) I'm so happy to be part of such an amazing church. My church and my Christian friends. . .they mean the world to me. I want to pay close attention so I can find out when people are in need. I don't want to find out after the fact that my friend's family was in need and no one came to help. I want to be the one! So open my ears, Lord. Help me hear. Open my eyes. Help me see. I don't ever want to overlook a friend who's going through a rough season. I want be the kind of friend to offer a shoulder. . . and a hand. Amen.

Be the Change
Talk to members of your church about setting up a phone
tree system to spread the word when crises happen.

CARING FOR ORPHANS AND WIDOWS

Religion that is pure and undefiled before God the Father is this: to visit orphans and widows in their affliction, and to keep oneself unstained from the world.
JAMES 1:27 ESV

This is the proof that I love You, Lord, that I want to take care of orphans and widows. The Bible makes it clear, You care a *l-o-t* about this one! I don't always remember. I don't always remember to be extra nice to the kids who don't have a dad or to the elderly people at my church who are widows. Thanks for reminding me through this verse that You care about those who can't take care of themselves. You're a defender of the weak, and You're making me want to be a defender too. May I stand up for them when others seek to bring them harm. I want to help where help is needed, feed where food is needed, and provide care where care is needed. In other words, I want to step up and do the right thing so that these awesome people know they are never *ever* alone. Amen.

. . . .

Be the Change
Ask your parent if your family may be able to host Thanksgiving dinner for a widow or family in need.

CARING FOR THE ANIMAL KINGDOM

The righteous care for the needs of their animals,
but the kindest acts of the wicked are cruel.
PROVERBS 12:10 NIV

I'm an animal lover, Lord! I love puppies, kittens, hamsters, gerbils, fish, the list could go on forever! They make my heart so very happy! I know that many are mistreated or abandoned. This breaks my heart. Please give me creative ideas to help. Should I volunteer at my local shelter? Offer to walk the dogs? Clean out the kitties' cages? Bathe the pups? Should I ask my parents about adopting an animal in need? I know that You care very deeply about animals. The story of Noah and the Ark convinces me of that. So help me do my best to take care of the animal kingdom. I want to make Your heart happy. Amen.

. . . .

Be the Change
Offer to walk an elderly neighbor's dog.

PRAYER MOVES MOUNTAINS

*"Watch and pray so that you will not fall into temptation.
The spirit is willing, but the flesh is weak."*
MATTHEW 26:41 NIV

Father, Your Word tells me that prayer can move mountains. (Now, *that* would be a fun thing to watch!) When I pray, my words have power. There are many mountains in my life I'd love to see moved: not getting along with that kid in my math class, for instance. Or, not doing so well with my grades. So today I look those obstacles in the eye and say, "Be gone, in Jesus' name!" From now on, I'll pray in faith. I won't get discouraged by how big my problem is; instead, I'll tell my problem how big God is. When I speak in faith, I will encourage both myself and those around me. Situations can and will change with just a few faith-filled words. How I praise You for that! Amen.

. . . .

Be the Change
*Offer to pray in faith with a friend who's
going through a rough season.*

WE ARE ALL ONE

There is neither Jew nor Gentile, neither slave nor free, nor is there male and female, for you are all one in Christ Jesus.
GALATIANS 3:28 NIV

Father, this world is filled with billions of people, and most of them are nothing like me. Their homes are different, their foods are definitely different (and look a little weird, if you want the truth), the way they dress is even different. When I find out that some of them don't believe in You, I get nervous. How can I convince them? It seems impossible. Your Word says that I'm to go into all the world and preach the gospel. I don't know how far I'll ever be able to travel until I'm older, but one way I can impact the lives of people all around the globe is by praying for them. Today I choose to pray that people of all nations will be won to You, Lord. May the whole earth praise the name of Jesus. Amen.

. . . .

Be the Change
Pray daily for people of every tribe, nation, and tongue.

STICK CLOSE TO HIM

"If you abide in me, and my words abide in you,
ask whatever you wish, and it will be done for you."
JOHN 15:7 ESV

Lord, I know that one of the keys to receiving answers to my prayers lies in sticking close to You. I want to "abide" in You, Father. I want to spend time in Your presence, getting to know Your heart, Your will, Your plans for my life. I'm determined to have this very special relationship with You. Seems like it's easier to pray when I'm determined. It's also easier to believe You will do great things for me when I pray, because I know Your heart for me is good and not bad. So, today I ask in faith—for money for those in need, for healing for the sick, for a bright future for all the people I know and love. I know these things will be done because I have chosen to stick close to You. Praise You, Father. Amen.

Be the Change
Offer to help decorate a friend or loved one's house.

PRAYING FOR MIRACLES

He replied, "If you have faith as small as a mustard seed, you can say to this mulberry tree, 'Be uprooted and planted in the sea,' and it will obey you."
LUKE 17:6 NIV

I love this promise from the Bible, Lord! Sometimes my faith really is as small as a mustard seed—a teensy-tiny drop of faith is all I can find! But Your Word says that is enough. It doesn't take much faith to see miracles take place! With just a drop of faith I can look at hard things and command them to go. Fear, be gone! Doubt, be erased! Worry, you have to go. Anger, get lost! All of these and more have to flee at the name of Jesus. So, today I pull out my mustard seed faith. I look my problems in the eye and say, "Get out of here!" Then I watch them take a flying leap! Amen.

. . . .

Be the Change
Keep a careful eye out for God's miracles; share what you see with your friends for faith-boosting encouragement!

YOUR SPIRIT PRAYS THROUGH

Likewise the Spirit helps us in our weakness. For we do not know what to pray for as we ought, but the Spirit himself intercedes for us with groanings too deep for words.
ROMANS 8:26 ESV

I don't always know how to pray, Lord. Some times are harder than others: The day my friend's grandma died. That time the kids in my class made me feel left out. That time I wondered if my friend's mom had enough food in her house to feed her kids. During those times, when I got really scared, Your Spirit began to pray through me, uttering thoughts so deep, so intense, that I knew the words could not be my own. You know just what to say, even when I don't. You know just what to do, when I have no clue what to do. You know just how to stand, even when I feel like crumbling to the ground. You're my everything, Lord, and I'm so grateful to You. Amen.

. . . .

Be the Change
Use your words for good. Send letters of appreciation to men and women in the military.

81

PRAYER TO FACE YOUR ENEMIES

Be brave when you face your enemies. Your courage will show them that they are going to be destroyed, and it will show you that you will be saved. God will make all of this happen.
PHILIPPIANS 1:28 CEV

Sometimes I feel like such a coward, Lord. When kids around me start arguing, I just want to run away. I would rather crawl in a hole than face my enemy. But You're teaching me to be brave, Lord, especially when it comes to praying for those who oppose me. You're giving me the courage I need to stand up to the bullies and to make an impact. . .all through the power of Your love. I'm also learning to pray for those who hurt me, even though it's not easy. When I take the time to do this, everything changes. I begin to see them through Your eyes, and that's the best way to see anything! Thanks for giving me courage, Father. Amen.

Be the Change
Pray for those who have hurt you.

ACCOMPLISH ALL THE GOOD THINGS

So we keep on praying for you, asking our God to enable you to live a life worthy of his call. May he give you the power to accomplish all the good things your faith prompts you to do.
2 THESSALONIANS 1:11 NLT

You've got a lot for me to do, Father. I can feel it! There are big things coming in my life. Sometimes I wonder how I'll find the time or energy to accomplish it all. Then I'm reminded of all You've brought me through already. I know with Your help I can do anything. Today, I will pray over the things that are coming, the things I can't see yet. Prayer will make my faith grow and give me courage to step out when the time comes. I know that You'll give me the power I need to accomplish *all* the good things You've placed in my heart, but that power comes when I take the time to pray. I want You to be happy with the life I live, Lord. Amen.

. . . .

Be the Change
Keep a written list of all the ideas God is giving you. Be ready to take action when God calls.

IN SECRET

"But when you pray, go into your room and shut the door and pray to your Father who is in secret. And your Father who sees in secret will reward you."
MATTHEW 6:6 ESV

I don't want to be a bragger, Lord. I don't want to go around telling everyone what a great Christian I am. If I'm being honest, I mess up almost as many times as I do things right. That's why I love hanging out with You. You meet me in the secret places for a quiet chat—in my bedroom, sitting in my favorite chair, or on a walk through the park. You love to spend quiet time with me. No jumping up and down. No shouts of celebration. Just pure, sweet, secret time—where I pour out my heart and You wrap Your loving arms around me and whisper, "Peace, be still! It's going to be all right." Oh, how I love our secret times together, Father. Amen.

. . . .

Be the Change
Choose a favorite "prayer chair" where you can meet daily with God. Pray for your loved ones.

NO MORE KNOW-IT-ALL!

"Call to me and I will answer you and tell you great and unsearchable things you do not know."
JEREMIAH 33:3 NIV

Sometimes I feel like a know-it-all, Lord. I guess I want to show off to people and make them think I'm amazing. But You know better. All I am, all I have, all I will ever be is because of You. I can only accomplish what You place in my heart. Big or small, every task is from You. And You're preparing things for my life-journey, even now, that really would blow me away if I knew all of it. I have to keep trusting that You will show me what to do. I know You wouldn't call me to do big stuff if You didn't plan to show me how. My journey with You is such an adventure, Lord! Amen.

. . . .

Be the Change
Write down your story of being saved—think about where you started. That way, you'll never forget all the ways God has used you and improved you.

THE SPIRIT IS WILLING

"Watch and pray that you may not enter into temptation. The spirit indeed is willing, but the flesh is weak."
MATTHEW 26:41 ESV

I have to be on my guard at all times, Lord. Just about the time I think my faith is stronger than ever, I'm tempted to do the wrong thing and I fall right into the enemy's trap. Ugh! These moments make me feel like such a spiritual loser. Thank goodness You don't think I'm a loser! No way. Even when I've really messed up badly, You give me a pat on the back and say, "Get up, kid! Keep going!" If You didn't do that, I might just give up. I need You so much after I take a tumble, Father. My spirit is willing to go wherever You call, but my flesh is weaker than I'm willing to admit. So I'll keep watching. I'll keep praying. Eyes wide open, so that the enemy won't get his foot in the door! Amen.

Be the Change
Write down verses of encouragement from the Bible to pull out and read when you need them the most.

TRANSFORMED

I appeal to you therefore, brothers, by the mercies of God, to present your bodies as a living sacrifice, holy and acceptable to God, which is your spiritual worship. Do not be conformed to this world, but be transformed by the renewal of your mind, that by testing you may discern what is the will of God, what is good and acceptable and perfect.
ROMANS 12:1–2 ESV

Oh, I know what "transformed" means! I have toys that transform from one thing to another. They look a certain way, then I move a few things around and they look completely different. To transform means something changes. That's what You want to do in my life, Lord! You want me to be willing to change, to give up my selfishness, my sins, my ugly words, my disrespect, my complaining. You want to change my thinking, to make me more like You. I'm okay with that! To be honest, I get a little tired of doing things my way. So, transform me today, I pray. Amen.

Be the Change
Get out of your comfort zone! Host a Bible study for your friends in your home.

LOVE YOUR ENEMIES

"But I tell you, love your enemies and pray for those who persecute you."
MATTHEW 5:44 NIV

This is a tough one, Lord. I usually just want to talk badly about my enemies or get even for the things they've done to hurt me! But I know Your ways are higher than my own. You're teaching me how to pray for my enemies, even for those who've talked about me behind my back or made fun of the way I look or dress. You're even showing me how to forgive those who roll their eyes when I start talking about believing in You. You want me to pray for everyone—the good, the bad, and the ugly. Even the meanest kid in class. So, today I promise to do that. I will start with the ones who have hurt me or said bad things about people I love. Help me, I pray. Amen.

. . . .

Be the Change
Choose words that are kind, positive, and uplifting.

HEART, SOUL, AND MIND

Jesus replied: " 'Love the Lord your God with all your heart and with all your soul and with all your mind.' This is the first and greatest commandment. And the second is like it: 'Love your neighbor as yourself.' "
MATTHEW 22:37–39 NIV

It's not enough that I love You with my heart, Lord. I have to love You with my mind and my soul—my thoughts, my wishes, my dreams. My goals, my tomorrows, all the things I hope to be when I grow up. To truly love You means I have to trust that You're for me, not against me. I have to believe that loving You is the answer to any problem I might go through, any sticky situation I might face. When I love You, I find rest. I find comfort. I find peace. I find answers. You're truly all I need, Father. There is none like You, and I'm so grateful to be Your child. Amen.

. . . .

Be the Change
Make a list of all of your hopes, wishes, and dreams; then ask God how He feels about them.

GO TELL IT!

But you are a chosen race, a royal priesthood, a holy nation, a people for his own possession, that you may proclaim the excellencies of him who called you out of darkness into his marvelous light.
1 Peter 2:9 esv

You didn't choose me so that I could sit on the sofa and just enjoy Your love all by myself (though I have fun doing that, of course). You chose me, You called me, You gave me Your name, so that I could make a difference in the lives of people in my world. You didn't just do this to make Your kids feel special and included but to give us superhuman power to tell others about Your great love for us. When we share our stories of how You brought us out of tough stuff, people's lives are changed forever. There's great power in speaking up! So give me the courage to do that today, I pray. Amen.

. . . .

Be the Change
Ask a few friends to write down and share their testimonies of how God has delivered them out of darkness into His marvelous light.

GREAT ADVICE!

*Oil and perfume make the heart glad, and the sweetness
of a friend comes from his earnest counsel.*
PROVERBS 27:9 ESV

Sometimes I just need a friend who makes time for me, Lord. Most of my friends are crazy busy. They don't have time to come over and play or share a good, long chat. But that's what I really, truly want—a friend who takes the time. When we spend quality time together, it makes our friendship even better. We laugh. We talk. We share stories. We talk about the stuff we're going through (even the really hard stuff). He doesn't put me down or make me feel bad. He just listens and then shares his heart. He gives great advice too, and I really need that. I know it's because he really cares about me. I care about him too. Thank You for friends who take the time to share, Lord. Amen.

Be the Change
Offer to help your friend clean their messy bedroom.

A HEARTY LIFE

Whatever you do, work heartily, as for the Lord and not for men, knowing that from the Lord you will receive the inheritance as your reward. You are serving the Lord Christ.
COLOSSIANS 3:23–24 ESV

I'm not always a "hearty" worker, Lord. Sometimes I don't give it my best. I slink off into the shadows and hope that others will do the work I should've been doing. House-cleaning days are the worst! I'm low on energy. I don't have the "want to." But You're teaching me that serving You means I have to get with the program. I've got to do the work, no matter how hard. You'll give me the necessary energy—through Your Holy Spirit—to get the tasks done. And what cool tasks they are too! You want me to reach this world for You by living a godly life. So, I promise to work hard, so that I can lead others to You. I'll keep up the good work as best I can, Lord. Amen.

Be the Change
Mail a care package to a ministry or missionary with the help of a parent.

SHARING THE GOOD NEWS

For I am not ashamed of the gospel, because it is the power of God that brings salvation to everyone who believes: first to the Jew, then to the Gentile.
ROMANS 1:16 NIV

I'm not ashamed, Lord—not ashamed of the gospel, not ashamed of the life You've called me to, not ashamed to make Your name known throughout this earth. No hiding under a bushel for me! Nope! I'll let my light shine as bright as I can, even if others think I'm crazy. I'll shout Your good works to all who will listen. When I do this, people will see and hear, and they'll come to know You. Wow! People can be saved if I speak up. You've brought a lot of people into my life, Lord. Now, give me creative ideas to know where and when to share the good news of what You've done. I can't wait to get started! Amen.

. . . .

Be the Change
Share the gospel with a new friend.

THE NARROW GATE

"Enter by the narrow gate. For the gate is wide and the way is easy that leads to destruction, and those who enter by it are many. For the gate is narrow and the way is hard that leads to life, and those who find it are few."
MATTHEW 7:13–14 ESV

Do all roads lead to heaven, Lord? Does it really matter which god I serve? Won't I end up in heaven, anyway? That's what other people tell me. They say, "Why do you have to follow the Bible? It's a bunch of fairy tales!" But that's not true. Your Word is my sword! It's the truth. I have to face facts—there's only *one* way to heaven, and that's through Your Son, Jesus Christ. I'll share that message, no matter how unpopular, because it's the truth. It's a message that will change lives, which is what I want to do. I want to make a difference by shining bright, Lord! Help me as I speak up. Amen.

· ·

Be the Change
Speak the truth in love.

DO GOOD

*And do not forget to do good and to share with
others, for with such sacrifices God is pleased.*
HEBREWS 13:16 NIV

I've heard the phrase *do-gooder*, Lord. It's a person who does good deeds for others. I never thought of myself that way, but I kind of like the idea! I want to be known as someone who's generous, who cares more about the needs of others than personal wants and wishes. So, don't let me forget! Keep my eyes open so I can see kids who are hurting—in my neighborhood, my church, my school. I want to be there for people when they're going through stuff. I know You care deeply about those in need, Father. I want to care about them too and do good deeds as often as I can. Amen.

. . . .

Be the Change
*Send a "just because" card to a kid at school
who's going through a hard time.*

NO OTHER NAME

"And there is salvation in no one else, for there is no other name under heaven given among men by which we must be saved."
ACTS 4:12 ESV

There's so much power in the name of Your Son, Jesus, Lord! I love to speak His name. When I'm up against the greatest enemy, I just say the name of Jesus! When I'm sick and need healing. . . Jesus! When kids are talking about me behind my back or trying to make me mad. . .the name of Jesus calms me down. I could speak the name of every person I know, but none of them would save me. Even my favorite superhero can't do it! The name of Jesus brings power, life, and joy. Today, I choose to speak that name loudly, for all to hear. There is no other name by which mankind will be saved. Praise You, Jesus! Amen.

. . . .

Be the Change
Lay down your fears and speak the name of Jesus with boldness!

FOREVER FRIENDS

Jonathan said to David, "Go in peace, for we have sworn friendship with each other in the name of the Lord, saying, 'The Lord is witness between you and me, and between your descendants and my descendants forever.' " Then David left, and Jonathan went back to the town.
1 Samuel 20:42 niv

Some friends are just for a season and some last forever. I don't have a lot of "forever" friends, Lord, but a few will be with me for the rest of my life. I know that stuff changes—people move away. They go to different schools. They switch churches. Some even switch friends—replacing one for the other. But for now, I'm going to hang tight with my forever friends. They've been so awesome to get to know, and they've changed me in so many ways. I hope the same can be said in reverse. When it comes to changing the world, I plan to do it one friend at a time. And I guess this would be a good time to mention that You're my very best friend. I'm sticking with You till the very end. Amen.

. . . .

Be the Change
Make a list of your forever friends and pray for them daily.

BATTERY-CHARGING FRIENDSHIPS

*Therefore encourage one another and build
one another up, just as you are doing.*
1 THESSALONIANS 5:11 ESV

Some friendships wear me out and other friendships charge my batteries. I'll stick with the positive ones, Lord. Your idea of the perfect friendship is one that builds me up, not tears me down. I've had plenty of friends who wanted me to sink down to their level (misbehaving and lying). No thanks! Point me in the direction of godly people who will help me grow in my relationship with You. And while we're at it, let me just say that You're the most encouraging friend I've got! If I ever need cheering up, I just open Your love letter to me and start reading. The Bible is filled—cover to cover—with encouraging words. Thanks for that, Lord. Amen.

. . . .

Be the Change
*Offer to help an elderly neighbor
decorate a Christmas tree.*

FORGIVING FRIENDSHIP

*Make allowance for each other's faults, and forgive
anyone who offends you. Remember, the Lord
forgave you, so you must forgive others.*
COLOSSIANS 3:13 NLT

She hurt my feelings again, Lord. It's happened before, but this
time it *really* hurt. I know what Your Word says—I need to forgive
her. But what if it happens again? Okay, okay. . .I know I've done
things that need forgiving too. I'm not a perfect friend, either.
I mess up a lot. Help us figure this out, please? Show us how to
guard our tongues and how to forgive each other's faults. I want
to be quick to forgive, because I'm hoping people will be quick to
forgive me when I mess up. I can't help but think about the many
times You've had to forgive me, after all. You've shown me by
example what a true friendship looks like. I'm so grateful. Amen.

. . . .

Be the Change
Offer to hang out with a kid who's new at your school.

99

CLOSER THAN A BROTHER

A man of many companions may come to ruin,
but there is a friend who sticks closer than a brother.
PROVERBS 18:24 ESV

I've had a handful of "closer than a brother" friends in my life, Lord, and they're awesome! It's hard to imagine that anyone could be closer than an older brother or kid sister, but I've experienced it and know it's true. When I form a bond that tight, it's a real gift. We're on the same wavelength. We each know what the other is thinking and how they might respond to life's ups and downs. Best of all, I know for a fact that these friends aren't going anywhere, even if I mess up. They've got a real stick-to-it attitude and won't give up on me. I won't give up on them, either. They're worth the effort, Lord. Thanks for bringing them into my life. Amen.

. . . .

Be the Change
Surprise your BFF with an unexpected, well-thought-out gift.

IRON-SHARPENING FRIENDSHIPS

As iron sharpens iron, so one person sharpens another.
PROVERBS 27:17 NIV

She makes me better, Lord. Like iron sharpening iron, this amazing friend smooths off my rough edges and makes me a better human being. She's pretty good at speaking truth (and has hurt my feelings with her comments a time or two), but she's usually right on target with her words. I can't really be mad at her anyway, because she speaks with love and kindness, even when sharing hard stuff. That's why I adore her. I plan to keep her around for the long haul. I need someone like this, someone who wants to make me better. Show me how to sharpen her as well. Not in a hurtful way, of course, but in love—just like she does for me. Together, we'll grow stronger and stronger each day. Amen.

. . . .

Be the Change
*Offer to do chores with a friend just so
you can spend time together.*

101

UNTIL THAT DAY

I pray that your love will keep on growing and you will fully know and understand how to make the right choices. Then you will still be pure and innocent when Christ returns. And until that day, Jesus Christ will keep you busy doing good deeds that bring glory and praise to God.
PHILIPPIANS 1:9–11 CEV

Lord, You're showing me day by day how to make better choices. Sometimes I have to learn from my mistakes, but at least I'm learning! I can see growth in my spiritual life and I'm so glad. I'm finally figuring out how to say no to the bad stuff and yes to the good. I want, more than anything, to please Your heart. One of the reasons I'm trying so hard is because I know people are watching. They know I'm a Christian and they're curious to see if I am who I say I am (the real deal). I never want to be called a hypocrite. I want people to know that I really am who I say I am, whether I'm at home or in public. Amen.

- -

Be the Change
Offer to rake your neighbor's lawn.

TWO ARE BETTER THAN ONE

*Two are better than one, because they
have a good return for their labor.*
ECCLESIASTES 4:9 NIV

I've heard grown-ups say this, Lord: "Many hands make light work." I know it's true. When I've got a big task (cleaning out the garage, organizing my bedroom, sorting through clothes that no longer fit), I call on a friend to join me. She keeps me laughing and chatting as we work, and we get a lot done too! I know that two are better than one when it comes to prayer as well. There's a lot of power when two friends pray together! That's why I ask my friends to pray with me when I'm really going through bad stuff, because I know it makes my prayers even stronger! Thanks so much for blessing me with the kind of friends who will do this for me, Father. I want to be that kind of friend in return. Amen.

. . . .

Be the Change
Help a good friend sort through her giveaway clothes.

WALK WITH THE WISE

Walk with the wise and become wise,
for a companion of fools suffers harm.
PROVERBS 13:20 NIV

We become like the kids we hang out with. I know that's true, Lord. I've seen it happen in my own life. When I hang out with people who are lazy—who don't care about doing well in school—I become more like that myself. When I hang out with people who work hard, I end up working harder. It's easy to see that we rub off on each other! I need to spend time with people who will make me better, so give me friends who are a good influence. And while we're at it, make me a good influence as well. I don't want to rub off on people in the wrong way—by gossiping about others, wasting time, or giving in to temptation. May I learn from the wise and give off wisdom in return. Amen.

. . . .

Be the Change
Help a friend on moving day.

GOD'S INTIMATE FRIENDSHIP

"Oh, for the days when I was in my prime,
when God's intimate friendship blessed my house."
JOB 29:4 NIV

I've had lots of awesome friends, Lord—the kind I can share my heart with. These friends know when I'm going through a hard time (boy, do they know it!). They know when I'm struggling with temptation or headed in the wrong direction. I love these amazing friends. But You know who I love even more, Lord? You! You don't just know me in the way they do. You know me from the inside out. You know what makes me tick, why I behave the way I do, what my heart truly longs for. You're the most precious friend of all, because You cared enough to die in my place, that I could live forever. How can *any* friend ever top that? Oh, how I love You, Lord! Amen.

. . . .

Be the Change
Use your talents to bless someone.

UNSHAKEN

Therefore let us be grateful for receiving a kingdom that cannot be shaken, and thus let us offer to God acceptable worship, with reverence and awe.
HEBREWS 12:28 ESV

I've been through some tough stuff, Lord, as You know. Whew, it was rough! My knees were knocking and my hands were trembling. Even my voice quivered when I spoke. It really shook me up. But You were right there with me, Father. I came through everything okay, partly because of my attitude of gratitude. I'm learning that having a grateful heart is a real lifesaver when I'm going through stuff. Even when my feet are slug-bugging through a muddy path, I won't be shaken. I'll keep serving You, even when I'm going through bad times. I won't forget how You've brought me through in the past. I'll continue to praise You, even in the middle of the storm. Amen.

. . . .

Be the Change
Honor veterans in your community by thanking them for their service.

GROWING TOGETHER

*"And I tell you, you are Peter, and on this
rock I will build my church, and the gates
of hell shall not prevail against it."*
MATTHEW 16:18 ESV

There's nothing more awesome than spending time at church with my Christian friends, Lord! When I'm surrounded by people who are lifting up Your name in praise I feel warm and fuzzy inside. As we sing, as we worship, as we listen to Your Word, we're energized! We grow together, learn together, share together, pray together. All of it. . .together. And nothing can stop us, as long as we stick together. We're like a mighty army, ready to win the battle. How powerful we are, when we come together in Your name, Lord. I can't wait to grow up with these people! Amen!

. . . .

Be the Change
Volunteer to help in the church nursery.

KEEP WATCH OVER THE FLOCK

"Keep watch over yourselves and all the flock of which the Holy Spirit has made you overseers. Be shepherds of the church of God, which he bought with his own blood."
ACTS 20:28 NIV

I want to be a friend to those in need, especially inside my own church, Lord. Keep my eyes open wide, so that I don't overlook anyone who might be hurting. That kid next to me, the one with the sniffles? Maybe she's been crying because of something she's going through at home. Give me fun and creative ideas to care for the ones who need extra love—the elderly, the sick, the ones who need food, the single moms, the kids who feel left out and lonely. I want to be a friend to those who need a friend, so that no one feels like that. I'm so grateful for the times You surrounded me with Christian friends during my hard times, Father. Now I want to lift others up as I've been lifted up. Show me how, I pray. Amen.

. . . .

Be the Change
Look for a need today and meet it however you can.

LET'S GO TO CHURCH!

*And let us consider how to stir up one another to love
and good works, not neglecting to meet together, as
is the habit of some, but encouraging one another,
and all the more as you see the Day drawing near.*
HEBREWS 10:24–25 ESV

Honestly, Lord, some Sundays I don't feel like getting out of bed. I don't want to go to church. I want to pull the covers over my head and sleep longer, or maybe hang around in my pj's watching shows on TV or playing video games. But You've shown me how different my day can be when I go to church, even when I don't feel like it. Being there brightens up everything! Suddenly I'm not lazy anymore. I have so much energy, I feel like I could change the world! So don't let me give in to the temptation to stay in bed when I should be up. Going to church will be awesome, especially because I can hang out with friends and worship You with my whole heart. Amen.

. . . .

Be the Change
*Give someone at church a big hug and tell
them how much they mean to you.*

TWO OR THREE

"For where two or three gather in my name, there am I with them."
MATTHEW 18:20 NIV

A church doesn't have to be huge to make a difference in the world, does it, Lord? The Bible says that even two or three people (even kids!) can change the world when they link their hearts, minds, and prayers. Wow! That's amazing to think about. This is why going to church is so important. You don't want anyone to be alone. We all stick together like glue, and we're like a wall that can't be knocked down! You're right there with us when we gather together, Lord. What an amazing promise, that the God of the universe would come to church with us and join us as we worship! This knocks my socks off, Lord! Amen.

. . . .

Be the Change

Working with the other kids (and teachers), offer to host a Sunday lunch for the moms at church.

GIFTS TO BUILD THE CHURCH

What then, brothers? When you come together, each one has a hymn, a lesson, a revelation, a tongue, or an interpretation. Let all things be done for building up.
1 CORINTHIANS 14:26 ESV

I love how You work, Lord! You give different gifts to different people. One person sings. Another plays the piano. Another knows how to write or act or be a good leader. Another teaches a class for senior citizens. Another enjoys praying with the sick. Another loves to work in the church's nursery taking care of the kids. There's a slot for everyone to fill, no matter what they enjoy. And I've been paying attention when I'm at church. . .there's a lot of work to be done! Thanks for showing us that each one can play a role. I'll never feel left out, as long as we work together! Thanks for including me! Amen.

Be the Change
Offer to help with the toddlers' Sunday school class.

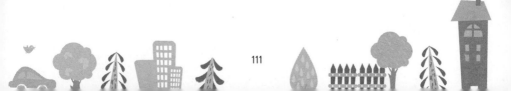

GOOD GIFTS

To equip the saints for the work of ministry,
for building up the body of Christ.
EPHESIANS 4:12 ESV

Your Word says that You give gifts to all of Your kids, Lord. It's easy to see when I look around me, but sometimes I wonder what gifts You're growing in me. What will I be when I grow up? What talents will I have? Will I teach a class? Sing in the choir? Help in the church office? Print newsletters? Cook meals for church dinners? Provide entertainment for outreaches and big events? Help out with the church's website? There are so many areas where I might fit in, but I'm not sure yet because I'm not there yet. I just know that You've got cool things planned for my future, and You want to use me in my local church body. I can hardly wait to see where I'll end up, Lord, but I trust You with the process. Amen.

. . . .

Be the Change
Make a list of things you like to do now, and come
up with roles you might enjoy when you're older.

GETTING ALONG

*For we were all baptized by one Spirit so as to form
one body—whether Jews or Gentiles, slave or free—
and we were all given the one Spirit to drink.*
1 CORINTHIANS 12:13 NIV

People don't always get along, do they, Lord? I've seen all the squabbling and fighting between my friends, and it's not pretty! It's almost like some people are deliberately putting up walls to keep others out. I hope nothing like that ever happens at my church. We're all brothers and sisters, and we love each other! No matter where we came from, no matter our color or background—we are one in You. You've stitched us together like my grandma's colorful quilt. That quilt wouldn't be the same if we were all identical. The people at my church are all different, but that's what makes us special. Thanks for these amazing people, Lord. Amen.

. . . .

Be the Change
Celebrate your pastor during Pastor Appreciation month.

i WAS GLAD

I was glad when they said to me,
"Let us go to the house of the Lord!"
PSALM 122:1 ESV

There are so many things I get excited about, Lord—ball games, family reunions, parties, celebrations, Christmas! As I count down the days, my excitement builds. I can hardly wait! That's how I feel about going to church on Sundays. With each day that passes, my heart hollers out, "It's coming! Sunday's coming, and I get to hang out with the people I love!" As I look at today's scripture I'm reminded that, even thousands of years ago, King David was super pumped over going to the house of the Lord. His heart was thumping with excitement! Not much has changed, has it? There's something so special about spending time at church, after all. Come on! Let's go! Amen.

. . . .

Be the Change
Ask someone new to sit with you during church.

ALL THINGS

And God placed all things under his feet and appointed
him to be head over everything for the church, which is his
body, the fullness of him who fills everything in every way.
EPHESIANS 1:22–23 NIV

Jesus, You're the top! You're the King of my life and the only Savior I will ever need. I can place all things under Your control— my heart, my thoughts, my mistakes, my pain, my sickness, that fight I had with my friend, that cranky teacher. You care about it all and want me to rest in You. So, today I choose to do just that. I won't wait until I'm sitting in church on Sunday morning. Right here, right now, I'll give You my broken heart, my tears, my pain, my broken friendships. Take them, I pray, and release me from any burdens attached to them. I'm so grateful I can trust You in *all* things, Lord. Amen.

. . . .

Be the Change
Ask a parent to take you to visit church
members who are sick or in the hospital.

COMMIT THEM TO THE LORD

And when they had appointed elders for them in every church, with prayer and fasting they committed them to the Lord in whom they had believed.
ACTS 14:23 ESV

This is really cool, Lord! When men and women are called into service for You, everybody in the church has a role to play. The Bible says that church members should gather around them, pray and fast, and then send them out to do the work. This act of sending people into service is precious. It reminds those being sent that they are not alone, and it reminds the ones who stay behind (like me!) that we have to keep praying for them, no matter where they are. I'm so grateful to my brothers and sisters who've listened to Your voice and answered Your call, Lord. May I always remember them in prayer, no matter where their ministry takes them. Amen.

. . . .

Be the Change
Put the photo of one who has been called into ministry on your refrigerator, where you can see it and pray daily.

CHANGE YOUR FAMILY, CHANGE THE WORLD

Your wife will be like a fruitful vine within your house;
your children will be like olive shoots around your table.
PSALM 128:3 NIV

Lord, I'm so blessed to have my family. When I look around at all of the loved ones who make up my world, I am so excited and grateful! Mothers, fathers, brothers, sisters, aunts, uncles, cousins, and close friends who might as well be family. . .I love them all. I think it's awesome that You've given me these amazing people to grow up with. I always want them to know how much I care, especially the little ones. They're looking up to me as an example, after all. I don't ever want anyone in the family to turn away from You because of my poor actions or behavior. If I can change my family and turn their hearts toward You, then I can change the world. My family will do awesome things for You, Lord. How amazing! Amen.

. . . .

Be the Change
Ask a family member to spend the day with you doing
something fun like bowling or going to the park.

CRAIN UP A CHILD

Train up a child in the way he should go;
even when he is old he will not depart from it.
PROVERBS 22:6 ESV

I've been looking at this verse for a while now, Lord. You gave me to my parents to raise and they're doing a good job. But, man! It's a *big* job. I don't always make it easy on them, I confess. They're doing their best to train me to love You. They've taught me Your Word, shown me how much You love me, and even helped me give my heart to You. I love the promise in this verse that a child who's been trained in Your ways won't depart from You when he or she is old. I'm claiming that promise for myself, Lord, and for the children I may one day have. I don't ever want to hold anyone back. I want to be a positive, uplifting trainer, one who shows people what the Father-heart of God looks like. Amen.

. . . .

Be the Change
Ask a parent to help you host a kids'
Bible study group in your home.

ONE FATHER

For this reason I bow my knees before the Father,
from whom every family in heaven and on earth is named.
Ephesians 3:14–15 esv

Lord, it's amazing to think that I'm connected to every single family on planet earth through You, my heavenly Father. I have brothers and sisters I'll never meet in this life, but we'll get to know each other in heaven. That's so cool! Christians around the world all worship the same God (You!), and they all praise the name of Your Son, Jesus! No matter what language we speak, how we dress, what foods we eat, or the color of our skin, we are connected through You, Lord! How can I ever thank You for including me in Your family? What a blessing, to love and be loved by so many of Your kids. Amen.

. . . .

Be the Change
Become a pen pal with a fellow believer in a different country.

AS CHRIST LOVED THE CHURCH

*Husbands, love your wives, just as Christ loved
the church and gave himself up for her.*
EPHESIANS 5:25 NIV

Lord, I can't even imagine how much Your Son, Jesus, loves us. Wow! His love runs so deep that He was willing to lay down His life for us. I've never known this kind of love before. I mean, I know that my parents would do anything for me, and my grandparents too. . .but to sacrifice their lives? I can't imagine it. The Bible says we're supposed to show that sort of love to those within our own families. What a difference it would make if we offered sacrificial love to our kid brother or older sister. We really could make a difference, because they would start to love others too. Before long, the whole world would be filled with loving people. We could change the world! Help us do that, I pray. Amen.

. . . .

Be the Change
Offer to do someone else's chores.

A LONG AND HAPPY LIFE

Children, you belong to the Lord, and you do the right thing when you obey your parents. The first commandment with a promise says, "Obey your father and your mother, and you will have a long and happy life."
EPHESIANS 6:1–3 CEV

What an amazing verse, Lord. If it's really true that obeying my parents will lead to a long and happy life, then I don't want to mess this up. I want to get it 100% right! I know my parents will be excited to hear this news. They've been wanting me to obey for a long time! I want to make sure all the kids I know understand this promise too, so that they can live long and prosperous lives also. This is the first commandment with a promise, as Your Word says, but that doesn't mean obeying my elders comes easily. Sometimes it's really hard. But You will help me with that, I know, because You want me to have an amazing life. Amen.

. . . .

Be the Change
In the future, be sure to obey the first time your parents tell you to do something.

YOU AND YOUR HOUSEHOLD

And they said, "Believe in the Lord Jesus, and you will be saved, you and your household." And they spoke the word of the Lord to him and to all who were in his house. And he took them the same hour of the night and washed their wounds; and he was baptized at once, he and all his family. Then he brought them up into his house and set food before them. And he rejoiced along with his entire household that he had believed in God.

ACTS 16:31–34 ESV

Father, thank You for including my household. You didn't just want my heart, You wanted the hearts of everyone I love—family members, from the oldest to the youngest. I pray for all of them, that they would walk with You forever and ever. May they serve You with joy and thanksgiving in their hearts. How happy I am to know that You loved us all so much that You adopted us into Your big family. Amen.

. . . .

Be the Change

Ask your parents questions about their parents.

YOU ARE MY PEOPLE

*Say to your brothers, "You are my people," and
to your sisters, "You have received mercy."*
HOSEA 2:1 ESV

It's a wonderful feeling, Lord, to live in such an amazing family. We don't always get along, but we love each other so much. I can look my brothers and sisters in the eye and say, "You're my people!" (Hopefully they feel the same way about me.) The best part is that we can forgive each other when we mess up. We can say, "I'm really sorry I borrowed your stuff without asking" or "Please forgive me for saying those mean things when I was angry." When we forgive, we have a clean slate, a fresh start. I also feel this way when I'm with my friends in church. Those people feel like family too! We're joined together by our faith. I wouldn't want it any other way, Lord. Thank You for blessing me with so many people to love (and forgive). Amen.

. . . .

Be the Change
If you've been holding a grudge, choose to forgive.

CARING FOR THE ELDERLY IN OUR FAMILIES

For the sake of my family and friends,
I will say, "Peace be within you."
PSALM 122:8 NIV

Lord, I love the elderly people in my family—the grandparents, parents, aunts, uncles, and so on. They're loaded with fun stories! Sometimes we laugh for hours when one of our grandparents starts talking about the good old days. Our family just wouldn't be the same without all of these amazing people. I've learned so much about how to live from those who are older (those who are still with us and those who have already passed on). Show me how to honor those in their golden years, to treat them with dignity and respect. Help me care for the ones in need with the tenderness they have always shown me. I want to bless them. . . and You, Lord. Help me, I pray. Amen.

. . . .

Be the Change
Plan an outing or a special event for
someone in their golden years.

FAMILY OF BELIEVERS

*Therefore, as we have opportunity, let us do
good to all people, especially to those who
belong to the family of believers.*
GALATIANS 6:10 NIV

I know we're called to treat all people with love and respect, Lord, but I'm glad You reminded me to be especially good to my church friends. I love them so much! The young ones, the older ones, the teachers, the singers, the preachers, the ones who play instruments, the ones who help in the office, the greeters, the janitors who clean the buildings. . .I think they're all awesome. And I know they love me too, because they tell me so. . .a lot. I get lots of hugs at church. (Oh boy, do those church people know how to hug!) Show me how to bring honor to the ones who've been so good to me and my family. I want to bless them for their years of service and love. Give me fun and creative ideas so that I can bring honor where honor is due, Lord. Amen.

Be the Change
*Spend an afternoon together with your church
friends making homemade ice cream.*

FOR HE IS GOOD

Give thanks to the LORD, for he is good;
his love endures forever.
PSALM 107:1 NIV

You are so good, Lord—to Your people, to all of creation. You're taking care of the little birds right now, aren't You? And I'll bet You're taking care of the elephants in Africa too! If You're willing to take care of animals, then for sure I can trust You with my life. Everything You do will be for my good because Your heart for me is good. I will never have to wonder if You're out to get me or mad at me when I make mistakes. Nope! That won't happen. You are for me, not against me. Even the best people I know sometimes slip up and do bad or unexpected things. When it comes to You, however, I know You won't let me down. I can count on You, my good, good Father. Amen.

Be the Change
Make a list of all the ways God has
shown you that He is good.

SPEAK IN FAITH

Now faith is confidence in what we hope
for and assurance about what we do not see.
This is what the ancients were commended for.
HEBREWS 11:1–2 NIV

Faith. What an awesome word! Faith gives me the courage to step out and do the impossible. When I learn to speak in faith, to completely trust You, Lord, I feel courageous. I'm like a superhero, ready to take on any challenge. I can pray in faith, believing for miracles. Faith gives me super-confidence—it makes me sure of things that haven't even happened yet. I can pray for the sick and hope for great news! I want to be like the great men and women in the Bible who were rewarded for their great faith, Lord. I'm already on my way. I can't wait to witness Your great and mighty acts as I stand in faith and believe. Amen.

. . . .

Be the Change

Pray for a stranger who looks like they could use the
boost—maybe a restaurant server on a busy night,
or a mom with crying kids at the grocery store.

IF YOU HAVE FAITH

"And whatever you ask in prayer,
you will receive, if you have faith."
MATTHEW 21:22 ESV

"If." What a tiny little word, and yet, how powerful. I can have whatever I ask in prayer, Lord, *if* I have faith. There have been times I've asked for silly things, and I'm glad that You didn't say yes to all of the crazy stuff I wanted. But when it comes to the big stuff—praying for those in need—I want my "if" to be as solid as a rock. Make my faith strong! I want to see You move in supernatural ways. Talk about having some great stories to share! I want to come into my prayer closet with such an amazing faith that I walk out again, ready to witness miracles firsthand. I can't wait to see how You move, Lord! I have faith in You to do the impossible. Amen.

. . . .

Be the Change
Share your stories of faith with a new believer.

INCREASE OUR FAITH

The apostles said to the Lord,
"Increase our faith!"
LUKE 17:5 NIV

So many things have increased as I've gotten older, Lord—my height, my weight, my shoe size. The size of my jeans, my T-shirts. But there's one area of my life that I *really* want to see increase, Lord, and that's in my faith. Take my itty-bitty mustard seed of faith and blossom it into a whole tree. Stretch it. Grow it. Multiply it. May it be like a wildfire, out of control, growing faster than my hair, my feet, or the number on the scale! I want all You can give me, Lord, so do an amazing work in my heart and spirit, please. I'm going to grow, grow, grow in You, and I'm going to have a blast every step of the way. Amen.

. . . .

Be the Change
Make a list of ways you can strengthen your faith.

THE WORD GOES FORTH

"So shall my word be that goes out from my mouth; it shall not return to me empty, but it shall accomplish that which I purpose, and shall succeed in the thing for which I sent it."
ISAIAH 55:11 ESV

There's power in Your Word, Lord! Wow, have I ever learned this firsthand! When I speak the words from the Bible out loud, I'm speaking Your heart, Your will, Your love. Those words cover everything I'm going through, even the hard things. They bounce back empty. If I speak peace into a situation, I can expect peace to come back to me. If I speak healing, I believe for healing. The words have power, not because of anything I've done, but because of who You are. Thank You for giving us Your Word, Lord. It is a powerful weapon in my hands, one I'm so grateful for. Amen.

. . . .

Be the Change
Write down scriptures and post them around your house. Speak the words aloud as often as possible so that you can commit them to memory.

FAITH IN HIS NAME

*"By faith in the name of Jesus, this man whom you
see and know was made strong. It is Jesus' name
and the faith that comes through him that has
completely healed him, as you can all see."*
ACTS 3:16 NIV

The name of Jesus changes everything! At that name, nations
bow. The devil runs and hides behind the nearest tree! Bad stuff
changes to good. Wicked people turn their lives around and start
living right. The name of Jesus is one I love to speak, Lord! I cry
out, "Jesus, come and fix this, please!" or "In the name of Jesus,
anger has to leave!" There's power in that name—power to make
change in the life of someone who's in pain. Without that name,
I don't know where I'd be. Lost, for sure! Oh, but everything in
my life has changed because of that amazing name. Amen!

. . . .

Be the Change
*Speak the name of Jesus over a situation
you're currently going through.*

BY FAITH, WE UNDERSTAND

*By faith we understand that the universe was
created by the word of God, so that what is seen
was not made out of things that are visible.*
HEBREWS 11:3 ESV

There are things I'll never understand, Lord—why some kids lie and cheat, how one person can bully another, why anyone would turn away from You and return to a life of sin. It's really hard to figure that one out, Lord, because they once claimed to love You. Then they turned away. But You're helping me see with spiritual eyes. There's a real enemy (the devil), and he tempts us. Lots of people fall right into his trap. But I don't want to do that! That's why it's more important than ever for me to stick close to You and to ask for Your way of doing things. Thank You for giving me eyes to see what's really going on out there. I'm going to be on my guard, so I will always understand what's happening around me. Amen.

. . . .

Be the Change
Keep your spiritual eyes open.

DOUBT, A TROUBLESOME WEASEL

*"Truly I tell you, if anyone says to this mountain,
'Go, throw yourself into the sea,' and does not
doubt in their heart but believes that what they
say will happen, it will be done for them."*
MARK 11:23 NIV

I'll be doing just fine, Lord, and then. . .bam! Doubt slips in. Five minutes ago, I was filled with faith. I could move mountains! I could pray in faith. Now I'm feeling like a coward. I can't even find one ounce of faith. Where did it go? How did it disappear? How quickly I forget the things You've done before. I want You to grow my faith, Lord, till it's so strong that doubt can't weasel its way in. I want the kind of faith that looks at obstacles as small hurdles, not big mountains. Doubt be gone, in Jesus' name! I've got work to do, and you're in my way! Amen.

. . . .

Be the Change
*Write the words "Pray and Don't Doubt" on a slip
of paper and post it on your bathroom mirror.*

THE POWER OF THE TONGUE

Death and life are in the power of the tongue,
and those who love it will eat its fruits.
PROVERBS 18:21 ESV

I've heard it all my life, Lord—the power of life and death is in the tongue. I don't pause to think about that phrase, but it's so true. It's my choice, and I need to choose wisely. I can lift people up or tear them down with my words. I can encourage other students or bring discouragement. . .all with my words. I can heal a friendship or cause pain so deep it's not fixable. . . all with the power of my tongue. My choice today (and always) is to speak life into situations, to be known as one who shares positive thoughts, uplifting words. I don't ever want to be caught speaking badly of people or cutting them down. May this tongue only be used to speak life. Amen.

Be the Change
Brag on someone you know who's overcome an obstacle.

LET THERE BE LIGHT!

And God said, "Let there be light," and there was light.
GENESIS 1:3 ESV

With just a few words from You, Lord, the earth was formed. Light split the darkness. Animals were created. Man was formed out of the dust. Woman was made from man's rib. You spoke, and things happened instantly. Nothing has changed, Lord. You're the same—yesterday, today, and forever. And You're still speaking. You speak life over scary situations I go through. You speak peace to my heart whenever I'm troubled. You speak healing when I'm in pain. Your words are as powerful today as ever. I know, because I've experienced them in my life many times. You spoke into my heart, and my life was changed forever. I praise You for Your spoken words! Amen.

. . . .

Be the Change
Help a friend who may be scared of the dark.
Let them know Jesus is the Light of the world!

CALLING THINGS INTO EXISTENCE

As it is written, "I have made you the father of many nations"—in the presence of the God in whom he believed, who gives life to the dead and calls into existence the things that do not exist.
ROMANS 4:17 ESV

During Creation week You spoke all sorts of things into being—giraffes with long necks, woodpeckers, dogs, cats, hyenas, hooting owls, koala bears, mice, ants, mountains that touched the sky, raging rivers, tall trees, grains of sand, and so much more. I love Your imagination, Father! I want that same kind of creativity so that when I speak life into my situations, amazing things happen. How awesome You are to put so much power into my words, Lord! I'm so glad I can speak into the darkness and see light. Amen.

. . . .

Be the Change
Draw or paint a picture of what you imagine Creation was like. Share it with your family.

AN ATTITUDE OF GRATITUDE

This is the day that the Lord has made;
let us rejoice and be glad in it.
PSALM 118:24 ESV

You give me so many choices, Lord. You don't force me to do anything. Should I sit around and whine about all the things going wrong in my life, or speak in faith over them? Speak faith, of course! You've come through for me in the past. I want to have an attitude of gratitude, even when I'm going through rough stuff. The Bible tells me to be positive, even when I'm going through bad things. I know there's power in praise, so today I choose to speak powerful words of thanksgiving, no matter what I'm walking though. You've been so good to me, Lord. How could I help but praise Your name? Amen.

Be the Change
Make a list of the top ten things you're thankful
for, then praise God for every item on the list.

OBEDIENCE

He must manage his own family well and see
that his children obey him, and he must do
so in a manner worthy of full respect.
1 TIMOTHY 3:4 NIV

Sometimes I wonder if some of the kids in my class will ever learn to obey our teacher, Lord. She has to get on to them a lot, but it doesn't seem to make much difference. They just keep on being disobedient. They get into all sorts of trouble on the playground, in PE class, and even while we're waiting for the bus! Just about the time I start to give up on them, I remember how patient You've been with me, how many times You've had to calm me down or correct me. I'm not exactly perfect, either. I'm so grateful for Your forgiveness, Father. Thanks for giving second chances. I want to be just as caring with others—whether they're kids at school, at church, or in my neighborhood. Show me how, I pray. Thank You, Lord. Amen.

Be the Change
Offer to help your teacher.

PRAYING FOR YOUR FRIENDS

After Job had prayed for his friends, the Lord *restored his fortunes and gave him twice as much as he had before.*
JOB 42:10 NIV

I read about this man named Job in the Bible, Lord. Wow, he went through a *l-o-t* of bad stuff. I can learn a lot of lessons from his story, but here's one I never thought of till now: You didn't turn Job's life around until *after* he prayed for his friends. Sometimes I wonder why You're taking so long to answer my prayers. Maybe You're just waiting on me! Maybe it's time for me to lift up a prayer for my friends so that You're free to move. I hadn't thought about that before! I want to be someone who really prays for others, not just during rough seasons, but every single day. Thanks for the reminder that praying for my friends is a blessing and an honor. Amen.

Be the Change
Make a list of friends who are in need of prayer right now.

WHERE YOUR TREASURE IS

*"For where your treasure is,
there your heart will be also."*
MATTHEW 6:21 NIV

When I look at some of the grown-ups in my neighborhood, I see the things that they care about: Cars. Houses. Money. Jobs. Relationships. These things are important, but some people have made these things their treasures. They don't get it, do they, Lord? You're the only treasure that any of us will ever need. You are our all in all, our everything. You're more valuable than anything we could ever own. When we put You in Your proper place (on Your throne), You give us everything else we need. Thanks for the reminder, Father. Where my treasure is, there my heart will be. May I never forget! Amen.

Be the Change

*Give away some of your clothes or toys (earthly treasures)
to a local charity. Remember God is our forever treasure.*

NEVER CEASE

*I do not cease to give thanks for you,
remembering you in my prayers.*
EPHESIANS 1:16 ESV

Sometimes I feel like a yo-yo, Lord! I'm up one minute, down the next. I praise You one day, then moan and groan the day after. That's one reason I'm happy for this reminder from Your Word that You want me to always give thanks to You. May I never stop, even on the hard days. My praise is even more powerful when I'm going through a rough season. So, today I say, "Praise the Lord! Thanks for all You've done, all You're doing, and all You plan to do." I really am grateful, Lord, even when I don't take the time to say it. I won't ever stop praising You, Father. Amen.

. . . .

Be the Change
*Write a letter of appreciation to God
for what He has done for you.*

MAKE HIM KNOWN

*Oh give thanks to the LORD; call upon his name;
make known his deeds among the peoples!*
PSALM 105:1 ESV

You've given me a special task, Lord—to share my praise, my thanks, my joy with all the kids I hang out with. It's like You've given me my very own microphone to carry. You want me to speak up. I have to tell others what You've done in my life. That time You healed me when I was sick with strep throat? I made You known. The time You came to my rescue when my best friend told me she hated me? I made You known. That time I felt depressed and didn't want to get out of bed? You restored my joy, so I made You known. I shared my story with everyone who would listen. I love to make You known, Father. Thanks for every opportunity. Amen.

. . . .

Be the Change
Think of creative ways to make God known today.

142

IMMEASURABLY MORE

Now to him who is able to do immeasurably more than all we ask or imagine, according to his power that is at work within us, to him be glory in the church and in Christ Jesus throughout all generations, for ever and ever! Amen.
EPHESIANS 3:20–21 NIV

You are an "above and beyond" Father. You don't just give Your kids what they need or what they ask for. You go above and beyond, giving us *w-a-y* more than we could ask or think. (Are You thinking up new ways to surprise me right now? What fun it must be, to come up with such creative ideas!) And it's all by Your power, not mine. That's such a relief! Why do You pour such goodness on me, Lord? To show Your glory, of course. People for years to come will share stories about the great things You've done. I'm so happy for what You're doing for me. Amen.

Be the Change
Go above and beyond: ask a parent to help you take baked goods to a local police station for the officers to enjoy.

IN ALL CIRCUMSTANCES

Give thanks in all circumstances; for this is
God's will for you in Christ Jesus.
1 THESSALONIANS 5:18 NIV

It's taken me awhile to figure this one out, Lord. You want me to praise You, to give thanks even when I'm feeling down in the dumps. I used to wonder if this was even possible. Now I know it is. There's something pretty awesome about stopping to worship and praise when I'm in a low spot. It takes my eyes off my problems and puts them onto You, the one with the answer. It lifts my spirits and reminds me that I have nothing to fear. So, I will go on giving praise, no matter what I'm facing. This is Your will for me—to lift up a song of praise in all circumstances.

. . . .

Be the Change
Give a listening ear to a friend who is
going through a rough season.

THE GOSPEL PROCLAIMED

"And the gospel must first be proclaimed to all nations."
MARK 13:10 ESV

Today my heart is with all of the missionaries in countries that are opposed to the gospel, Lord. I can't even imagine what they go through as they try to lead people to You, even when doing so is against the law. Guard and protect them, I pray. Open doors so that they are free to visit with the right people, those whose hearts are ripe for the gospel. Help their converts too. Give them peace, courage, and comfort as they start their new adventure with You in opposition to all around them. Please, God—protect them as they witness to others. I pray that Your Word spreads like wildfire in these countries and that the leaders will soon realize they must swing wide the gates for the gospel. Amen.

. . . .

Be the Change
Write a kind letter to a missionary who's struggling.

PRAISE LEADS THE WAY

Enter his gates with thanksgiving and his courts with praise; give thanks to him and praise his name.
PSALM 100:4 NIV

I remember a story from the Bible, Lord, about a man named Jehoshaphat. He entered into battle by putting his praise leaders on the front lines. They praised their way into the war and the battle was won, all because of praise. That's an amazing story! It reminds me that I need to praise my way into life's tough situations. If I'm going through stuff with praise and thanksgiving on my lips, then I'll stay encouraged. And I know my faith is set on fire (in a good way) by praise. Best of all, You love it when praise leads the way! No matter what I'm facing, I'll give a mighty shout and march to the front lines of the battle with the words "Praise You, Lord!" on my lips. Amen.

Be the Change
What "frontline" battles are you facing today? Praise your way into the battle.

VOLUNTEER LOCALLY

"In all things I have shown you that by working hard in this way we must help the weak and remember the words of the Lord Jesus, how he himself said, 'It is more blessed to give than to receive.'"
ACTS 20:35 ESV

Lord, I want to make a difference right here in my town. There are so many places that need help: homeless shelters, women's shelters, hospitals, and so on. Which ones should I help? Maybe I can choose one this month, and help another one next. I can ask my parents to take me to volunteer or ask my church to raise money to give them, Lord. Or maybe I should donate my old clothes and shoes. The possibilities are endless, and the need is great. I know I'm young, but if I put together a team of people—young and old—we can make a real difference. You've told me to help the weak and to remember (always) that it's more blessed to give than to receive. That really makes my heart happy, Father, so help me put this verse into practice. Amen.

. . . .

Be the Change

Ask a parent to help you learn more about volunteer opportunities that are right for you.

NURSING HOMES

Then he said to his disciples, "The harvest is plentiful,
but the laborers are few; therefore pray earnestly to the
Lord of the harvest to send out laborers into his harvest."
MATTHEW 9:37–38 ESV

Father, I know that a lot of older people live in nursing homes, but I don't know much about them. I want to help, but I don't know how. I'm just a kid, after all! Should I invite my church choir to sing Christmas carols during the holiday season? Should I make wreaths for the doors of the rooms? Should I offer to visit with a lonely patient who never gets visitors? Should I pray for the sick? Should I donate books or fuzzy slippers? There are so many things I could do. Help me put actions to my ideas. I want to help those who are feeling neglected, overlooked, or sad. Show me how to pray with them and share Your love with them in fun and creative ways. Amen.

. . . .

Be the Change

Send an encouraging card to someone your family
knows in a nursing home (relative or church member).

COMPASSION FOR LOCAL MISSIONS

Be kind and compassionate to one another,
forgiving each other, just as in Christ God forgave you.
EPHESIANS 4:32 NIV

Sometimes, Lord, I forget that there are hurting people all around me. Children at the local cancer hospital. Parents who are far from home, lonely and exhausted. Shut-ins unable to leave their homes or prepare their own meals. Caregivers taking care of elderly patients with memory loss. Parents caring for special needs kids. Soup kitchens in need of cooks. Animal shelters with dozens of pets in need of foster homes. Give me a heart for a local organization and then show me how to give of my time, talents, and treasures. I'm getting excited just thinking about the possibilities! Thanks for using me, Lord. Amen.

. . . .

Be the Change
Ask a parent to take you to the local
hospital to read to patients.

BEGIN AT HOME

*"And that repentance for the forgiveness of
sins should be proclaimed in his name to
all nations, beginning from Jerusalem."*
LUKE 24:47 ESV

Sometimes I see photos of little kids on the other side of the world—kids in need of food, medical care, and so on. It makes my heart sad, and I wonder what I can do to help. They seem so hopeless. You're showing me that I can bloom where I'm planted, Lord. There are needs right here in my own community. Sure, I want to make a difference in other parts of the world, but I have a feeling it might be a good idea to start close to home. Maybe when I'm older, I'll travel to other places. So, help me out, Lord! Show me how I can begin to share Your love with people in my neighborhood, my community, my town. Amen.

. . . .

Be the Change
Volunteer for or donate to a local Christmas toy drive.

GENTLENESS AND RESPECT

But in your hearts revere Christ as Lord. Always be prepared to give an answer to everyone who asks you to give the reason for the hope that you have. But do this with gentleness and respect.
1 PETER 3:15 NIV

Lord, I have to confess, I haven't always come across as gentle or respectful. Sometimes I jump into a situation, wanting to make a difference, but I insist on doing things my way. I don't want to wait on instructions, and I definitely want to be the leader, not a follower. I'm so excited about making a difference that I end up doing more damage than good. Only, You have different ideas. Oh, help! I don't ever want to be a nuisance or get in anyone's way, so slow me down and teach me how to respect those in charge. Help me be a great team player, always showing gentleness and respect to all, Lord. Amen.

Be the Change
Write a note of thanks to your school's lunch lady.

TO SEEK AND SAVE

"For the Son of Man came to seek and to save the lost."
Luke 19:10 NIV

Your Son, Jesus, came to save the lost people, Lord, and He didn't have to look very far to find them. I don't have to look very far, either. I don't have to cross oceans or travel by plane to find people who need to get to know You. They're all around me! My community is filled with people in need. Many need practical things—food, shoes, socks, medicine, care, shelter, and so on. Some need to hear Your gospel message and accept Jesus as Lord and Savior so that they can have a fresh start. You love all of these people so much, Lord. . .as much as You love me. And I want to love them too. Show me how to reach out to people around me, I pray. Amen.

. . . .

Be the Change
Sponsor a kite-flying day with kids in your neighborhood.

HE'S SENDING YOU

Jesus said to them again, "Peace be with you. As the Father has sent me, even so I am sending you."
JOHN 20:21 ESV

Father, You sent Your Son. You had an amazing plan for Him, one that would save mankind for eternity. Jesus left heaven—a place that was absolutely perfect with splendiferous mansions and dazzling streets of gold—to come to earth, where He had to go through hard stuff, persecution, and people turning their backs on Him. You're sending me too. I feel those nudges. You want me to step up and step out—to reach my neighborhood, my community for You. You're giving me God-sized ideas for how I can do that. I'm stepping out of my comfort zone, but I completely trust You, Lord. Where You send me, I will go, so point the way, I pray. Amen.

. . . .

Be the Change
Keep a list of the many ways God has called you out of your comfort zone to serve Him.

153

NOT TO CONDEMN

"For God so loved the world, that he gave his only Son, that whoever believes in him should not perish but have eternal life. For God did not send his Son into the world to condemn the world, but in order that the world might be saved through him."
JOHN 3:16–17 ESV

People can be so judgy, Lord! No wonder some people don't like to listen to Christians share the gospel message, because they do it in a mean way. Can You show me how to speak the truth in love? When I meet people who don't know You, I want to touch them with Your love and grace, to tell them how awesome You are! I want them to know that they can have eternal life and live forever in heaven with You someday. I know it won't always be easy to share. Some people really just don't want to hear it. I get that. But help me try anyway, Lord. What I can't do on my own, You can do through me. Thank You, Lord! Amen.

Be the Change
Work to be less judgmental toward people who are different from you.

POWER!

"But you will receive power when the Holy Spirit comes on you; and you will be my witnesses in Jerusalem, and in all Judea and Samaria, and to the ends of the earth."
ACTS 1:8 NIV

When I think about talking to others about You, Jesus, I start to get nervous! It's hard to reach out to the kid sitting next to me in school or the boy on the playground who's always picking on kids. I wonder how I can start the conversation. That's where Your Holy Spirit comes in. The Holy Spirit gives me power to speak—to the kids in school and anyone I meet along my journey. When I receive a heavenly reminder from the Holy Spirit, I'm filled with courage. No more hiding. I'll speak what I believe! I'm ready to jump right in! Something supernatural takes place. Thank You, Father, for sending Your Holy Spirit to empower me. I could truly never do this alone. Amen.

Be the Change
*Ask for the Holy Spirit to empower you to talk
to your classmates about Jesus today.*

DON'T GIVE UP

And let us not grow weary of doing good, for in
due season we will reap, if we do not give up.
GALATIANS 6:9 ESV

Sometimes I think of the farmers planting their seeds, Lord. They have to wait, wait, wait for the harvest to come. How patient they are! Me? I'm the opposite of that! I'm more impatient. I pray for a miracle and want it *now*. I talk to a friend about You and I want her to say, "I want to follow Jesus too" right away. I put food in the microwave and pull it out a minute later. But I'm working with Your clock now. Your Word promises that You will take care of things in Your time. I'm not sure when that will come, but I have Your promise that it will happen if I don't give up. So, I won't quit. I'll keep reaching out to those in need. Use me, even if I get a little impatient, Lord. Amen.

Be the Change
Host a "Back to School" backpack drive for local children.

FOREIGN MISSIONS

*"Therefore go and make disciples of all nations,
baptizing them in the name of the Father and of the
Son and of the Holy Spirit, and teaching them to
obey everything I have commanded you. And surely I
am with you always, to the very end of the age."*
MATTHEW 28:19–20 NIV

Lord, You told Christians to go into all the world. I think about missionaries who lived a hundred years ago. Traveling to foreign nations usually meant saying goodbye to friends and family forever, or at least for years at a time. What a sacrifice! I've thought about this verse a lot. I used to wonder if You wanted *all* of us to get on planes and move to places on the other side of the globe. I know now that You don't. Many people are supposed to stay right where they are. But I do think it's really cool that we have the internet now. I see my parents talking to people all over the planet. When I think about that, I get excited because I know that my mom and dad could spread the gospel from their computer at home. That's so cool, Lord! Amen.

Be the Change
Ask your parents about hosting a missionary in your home.

THE ENDS OF THE EARTH

"For this is what the Lord has commanded us:
'I have made you a light for the Gentiles, that you
may bring salvation to the ends of the earth.'"
ACTS 13:47 NIV

Lots of people across this great big world still haven't heard the gospel, Lord. I know the message is going out, but there are many who still haven't been reached. What can my family do to help? We can send our prayers, our money, even supplies. Anything they need, we can help from where we are. It's so cool to know we can make a difference, no matter where we live, Lord. So, introduce us to people who are making a difference. We want to connect with them and offer to help. Most of all, show us how to pray for those who are lost and for those carrying the message. Our hearts are with them all, Lord. Amen.

. . . .

Be the Change
Pray for children in a war-torn country who don't know Jesus.

PREACH THE GOSPEL

He said to them, "Go into all the world and
preach the gospel to all creation."
MARK 16:15 NIV

I've never thought of myself as a preacher, Lord. I don't always like getting up in front of my classmates at school to give presentations. Knowing everyone is listening to me makes me a little nervous. But I'm learning there are different ways to preach the gospel. I can share my faith with my classmates one-on-one by praying with them and talking about how awesome You are. You're not asking me to go to Bible college when I get older; You're just asking me to go when and where You call me. So, I open myself up to the possibilities, Lord. Use me to preach the gospel, Father. . .in whatever way You choose. Amen.

. . . .

Be the Change
Help other kids learn Bible stories and songs so
that they can share the gospel message.

IF THEY HAVE NOT HEARD

For, "Everyone who calls on the name of the Lord will be saved." How, then, can they call on the one they have not believed in? And how can they believe in the one of whom they have not heard? And how can they hear without someone preaching to them?
ROMANS 10:13–14 NIV

How often do I say things like, "Why don't they believe what I believe?" or "Why don't they just stop living in sin?" The truth is many people (even kids like me) are stuck in their ways because they simply haven't heard how to get out of it. I could be that person to tell them, Lord. With Your help, I could make a difference in the life of a person in my school or neighborhood. Show me how! No matter how You do it, I pray that I'm given the opportunity to reach out to someone with the gospel message, for it is life to all who believe! May all come to know You and be saved, Lord. Amen.

Be the Change

Spend time with a friend or family member you don't always get along with, and find an activity to do together that you both enjoy.

FOOD FOR THOUGHT

"I led them with cords of human kindness, with ties of love. To them I was like one who lifts a little child to the cheek, and I bent down to feed them."
HOSEA 11:4 NIV

I have all I need and more, Lord. When I open my pantry door, there's food inside. I don't have to wonder where the next meal is coming from; my parents make sure of that. I'm grateful for the way You provide for my family. Today I'm thinking about all of the many people across this planet who struggle to find food and water. I feel so small, Lord. I'm just a kid. What can I do to help? Remind me that even though I don't yet have a lot of money, I *do* have love and prayer. Father, I pray that help is given to those who need it most, and thank You for my own full belly. Amen.

. . . .

Be the Change
Ask a family member to help you plant a vegetable garden. Once the vegetables grow, you can donate them to a local soup kitchen.

ALL THE LITTLE CHILDREN
OF THE WORLD

Declare his glory among the nations,
his marvelous deeds among all peoples.
1 CHRONICLES 16:24 NIV

I remember the song, Lord, about how You love all the little children of the world. It brings amazing pictures to my mind—of little ones with different skin colors dressed in colorful clothes representing their countries. I may never travel to the places where these children live, but I can make a difference in other ways. I can become a pen pal and share my friendship and, more importantly, my love for You. My friends and I could go through our rooms and donate things to children in other countries: clothes we no longer wear, toys we don't play with, and books we no longer read. There are so many creative and helpful ways to play a role these days, and I want to do my best. . .that all the children of the world will come to know Your Son. Amen.

. . . .

Be the Change
Ask your teacher about setting up pen pals for
your class with kids in other countries.

SUPPORT A MISSIONARY

*Behold, upon the mountains, the feet of him who brings
good news, who publishes peace! Keep your feasts,
O Judah; fulfill your vows, for never again shall the
worthless pass through you; he is utterly cut off.*
NAHUM 1:15 ESV

I don't know how they do it, Lord. . .how some people pack their bags and move to far-off places like Zambia, Turkey, or Afghanistan to spread the gospel. I'm sure You're tugging on their heartstrings and they are responding to the call. Maybe when I'm grown-up I'll be a missionary. I don't know yet, of course. Or maybe I'll go on short missions trips, just to help. I like helping. I really do. The foreign mission field is huge and the workers are few. Thanks for getting me amped up about this, Lord! With Your help, I can make a difference in this world. Use me, Lord, I pray. Amen.

Be the Change
*Start saving money that you can send
to a missionary overseas.*

163

LIFT THEM UP!

Let the message of Christ dwell among you richly as you teach and admonish one another with all wisdom through psalms, hymns, and songs from the Spirit, singing to God with gratitude in your hearts.
COLOSSIANS 3:16 NIV

It feels good to be encouraged by my friends, Lord. I love it when they take the time out of their busy day to let me know how much they care about what I'm going through. Sometimes they give me little cards or notes that lift my spirit. This lets me know they're paying attention and that I'm not alone, which really helps. I want to be that kind of friend to others, one who notices what people are going through. I want to send little cards of encouragement and let others know that I'm praying for them and that I care. In other words, I want to be more like You, Lord. Help me, I pray. Amen.

Be the Change
Ask the Lord to point you in the direction of someone who needs your encouragement today.

AND THEN THE END WILL COME

*"And this gospel of the kingdom will be
preached in the whole world as a testimony
to all nations, and then the end will come."*
MATTHEW 24:14 NIV

I've read in the Bible that Your Son, Jesus, is coming back, Lord.
Is that going to happen soon (during my lifetime), or will it be
many years from now? No one seems to know for sure. One
thing is certain. . .I need to make sure my friends know about
You before that happens. I don't want any of them left behind.
No way. So, show me how to reach out to people, I pray. When
I'm in heaven I want to be able to look around and see lots of
people I know, people I shared the gospel with. How cool will
that be, to see people who are there because I was brave enough
to speak up! Thanks for using me, Lord. Amen.

Be the Change
Pray for a friend who doesn't know Jesus.

ALWAYS BE JOYFUL

Always be joyful. Never stop praying.
Be thankful in all circumstances, for this is God's
will for you who belong to Christ Jesus.
1 THESSALONIANS 5:16–18 NLT

If I really want to impact my world and make a real difference in the lives of the kids and adults around me, Lord, here's a good place to start! What if, from now on, I respond to every person, every situation, every tough challenge with joy? What if I never stop praying? What if I add thankfulness into my everyday life? What if I show gratitude every time someone blesses me? Wouldn't this be the best testimony ever, Father? I can almost picture it now. People would pass by me and say, "I'll have some of that joy too!" Joy is contagious, after all. Thanks for the reminder, Lord. Amen.

. . . .

Be the Change
Commit to joyful living, and be an example for others.

MAKE A JOYFUL NOISE

Let us come into his presence with thanksgiving;
let us make a joyful noise to him with songs of praise!
PSALM 95:2 ESV

I wouldn't say my singing voice is the best, Lord. Some days I only sing in the shower. (That's a safe place to rehearse!) But there are other days when I just want to sing out a song of praise to You—to make a joyful noise, no matter who's listening. I'm so glad You don't care about my singing ability. You're only worried about my heart. And my heart is fully in tune, Lord, a beautiful instrument pouring out music for You. When other kids hear me humming, when they see the smile on my face, I hope they ask, "Hey, what's up with you? You seem pretty happy about something today." I can't wait to share the story of why You've brought such joy, Lord. Amen.

. . . .

Be the Change
Start singing at least a little bit every day and
encourage your friends to join you.

JOY. . .COMPLETE!

"I have told you this so that my joy may be in you and that your joy may be complete."
JOHN 15:11 NIV

It feels really good when my mom's gas tank is filled to the tippy-top, Lord! I don't have any worries that we'll end up stranded on the side of the road. I feel safe. Comfortable. Excited for the journey. That's what it's like when my joy is filled to the top as well. When my joy is "complete," it spills over onto people around me. What makes me so joyful? The work You've done in my heart and life, Lord! And I know that others are watching. They're wondering what I'm up to because I'm smiling more than usual. I'll tell them, Lord. . .when the timing is perfect. Open doors for me to spread the joy, I pray. Amen.

. . . .

Be the Change
Go twenty-four hours without criticizing anyone (or anything).

SHOUT FOR JOY

*Be glad in the L*ORD *and rejoice, you righteous ones;*
and shout for joy, all you who are upright in heart.
PSALM 32:11 NASB

I'm not always the most joyous person, Lord. Ask any of the kids who hang around me when I'm in a bad mood. Ugh! But there are some times when I'm so full of joy, so excited about all You're doing in my life, that I want to lift up a shout of praise! "Hallelujah!" When this happens, I don't worry about what people are thinking! I'm ready to tell the whole world what You've done in my life—how You rescued me from sin and set my feet on a straight path. How You helped me forgive people who hurt my feelings. How You wiped away my loneliness and replaced it with godly friends who care. You've been so good to me, Father, and my heart can't help but praise! Now that's something to shout about! Amen.

- -

Be the Change
Find a quiet place and release a shout of praise to the Lord.
(Hint: your closet is an excellent place to praise Him!)

169

IN HIS JOY. . .I GO

*"The kingdom of heaven is like treasure hidden in a field.
When a man found it, he hid it again, and then in his
joy went and sold all he had and bought that field."*
MATTHEW 13:44 NIV

I love this story, Lord. A man stumbles across a treasure in a field that doesn't belong to him. He sells all he has to buy the field. Now the treasure is his! I can't even imagine how excited he must be! This story sticks with me because I feel like I found a treasure when I met You. I gave You all I had (my heart, my life) and You gave me access to the treasure, not just for now, but for all eternity. Heaven is my treasure! What a good and generous God You are. And how happy I am to be Your child. This great joy I'm feeling makes me want to go and tell others what You've done, so that they can experience this life-changing joy too.

Be the Change
Spend a few precious hours with someone who needs joy.

JOY COMES IN THE MORNING

For his anger lasts only a moment, but his favor lasts a lifetime! Weeping may last through the night, but joy comes with the morning.
PSALM 30:5 NLT

I go through happy seasons and sad seasons, Lord. I guess all kids do. Sometimes I think the tears will never end. I look at other people smiling when my eyes are flooded with tears and I wonder if I'll ever be happy again. I'm so glad the Bible promises that joy comes in the morning. Sad seasons don't last forever. Seasons of sadness will end, replaced by seasons of great joy. Your favor lasts for a lifetime. With the dawn of each new day I have an opportunity to start fresh, to choose joy, to rise above the pain. Thank You for the morning-born joy, Lord. It energizes and lifts me, just when I need it. What a blessing. Amen.

. . . .

Be the Change
Bring joy to a teacher by helping her set up her classroom.

ETERNITY IN YOUR HEART

He has made everything beautiful in its time. He has also set eternity in the human heart; yet no one can fathom what God has done from beginning to end.
ECCLESIASTES 3:11 NIV

You put it there, Lord. You set the desire to live forever in my heart. It was always Your desire to have us with you for all eternity. Long before Adam and Eve made a poor choice in the garden, You had this plan in motion—Your kids would be with You, not just in this lifetime, but the one to come. Sin tried to interrupt this plan, but Your Son, Jesus, came to fix that. Thank You! For those of us who place our trust in You, eternity is very real. I can't imagine the amazing things that wait for me in heaven, but I'm guessing it's all going to be pretty awesome. You've been working on eternity for, well, an eternity. Amen.

• •

Be the Change
Always keep heaven in mind. Share your thoughts about heaven with a friend.

A REFUGE OF JOY

*But let all who take refuge in you be glad; let them
ever sing for joy. Spread your protection over them,
that those who love your name may rejoice in you.*
PSALM 5:11 NIV

Our family has been through rough times, Lord. . .times that felt like they would never end. I can remember avoiding my friends when I was going through it because I didn't think they would understand. How could they? No one had been through it like we were going through it. During those dark seasons, You stayed right there with me, covering me from danger like a billowy cloud. You were my shelter, Lord, my hiding place. I'm so grateful for Your umbrella of protection. And look. . .everything changed! You turned my sadness into dancing. You turned tears into laughter. You provided just what I needed when I needed it. In short, Your presence changed everything, and I've never been the same. Praise You, Father! Amen.

· ·

Be the Change
Offer part of your lunch to someone who forgot theirs.

ALL JOY AND PEACE

*May the God of hope fill you with all joy and peace
as you trust in him, so that you may overflow
with hope by the power of the Holy Spirit.*
ROMANS 15:13 NIV

Here's a fun fact I love, Lord: joy and peace work hand in hand. When I'm fretting, I don't have joy or peace. But when I put my trust in You, when I count on You to handle the things I can't, then I'm at peace. Being at peace brings my heart such joy that I can't contain it. This is super obvious when You've rescued me from a tough situation or brought me through an illness. And You *love* doing this for me, Lord. Your Word says You want to fill me as I trust in You so that I can overflow by the power of Your Spirit. You do this on purpose—and I know it's because my joy has the power to change others. So fill me up, Lord! Amen.

Be the Change
*Talk about a fun way to bring joy! Why not swap
skills with an elderly neighbor? You can teach
each other how to do something new.*

HEAVEN REJOICES

"In the same way, there is more joy in heaven over one lost sinner who repents and returns to God than over ninety-nine others who are righteous and haven't strayed away!"
LUKE 15:7 NLT

Here's a fun scripture, Lord! Heaven throws a party when one sinner comes home to Jesus. A celebration takes place. Wow! What a party that must be! I can almost picture the angels high-fiving and the choir singing the "Hallelujah Chorus"! I'm excited to hear there's rejoicing in heaven, because I'm already in rehearsal now. I'm learning to receive and give joy wherever I go. I want people to know that You're my joy-giver! My heart overflows when I think about all You've done for me. Here's to an eternity of joy, Lord! Amen.

. . . .

Be the Change
Put on a play with your friends at a local retirement home.

AFFECT ETERNITY

*For God so loved the world that he gave his
one and only Son, that whoever believes in him
shall not perish but have eternal life.*
JOHN 3:16 NIV

It's kind of crazy to think that my actions today could affect eternity, but I know it's true. If I have a stinky attitude, it might cause someone to say, "Forget it! I don't want to be a Christian if that's what it's like." Or if I have a great attitude, my friend might say, "Yes! I want to be a Christian too!" This is one reason I desire to live a holy, godly life, because I know You want me to be a good witness while I have the chance. I don't want to waste a minute, Lord! Shift my focus from myself to others, from a life of selfishness to a life of giving. I want to spend a lifetime in heaven with the people I reach today. Amen.

. . . .

Be the Change
*Write down the names of people you hope
to reach for the Lord, and then come up with
possible ways to connect with them.*

HEAR AND BELIEVE

"Truly, truly, I say to you, whoever hears my word and believes him who sent me has eternal life. He does not come into judgment, but has passed from death to life."
JOHN 5:24 ESV

In order for my friends and family to spend eternity with You, Lord, they have to hear Your salvation message. Most of them know I'm a Christian, but I don't always know how to talk to them about it. (Isn't it strange that it's harder to reach out to my family members than total strangers, Lord? Why is that?) I want to make a difference in their lives, but it's such a careful balance when it's a good friend. Some of these kids really know how to push my buttons! But I won't give up. It's more important to me than anything, making sure those I love come to a saving relationship with You. Help me, I pray. Amen.

Be the Change
Be who you say you are, especially in front of family and friends. Make sure your actions and attitude match your faith message.

WHAT GOOD THING MUST I DO?

Just then a man came up to Jesus and asked,
"Teacher, what good thing must I do to get eternal life?"
MATTHEW 19:16 NIV

I'm a worker bee, Lord. Of course, You already know this. You created me, after all. When it comes to eternity, though, my hard work will never be enough to get me through heaven's door. I think about the story of the man who asked Jesus, "What good thing must I do to get eternal life?" He was a lot like me, I guess. . .looking to himself for answers. Jesus gave him a lot to think about, especially when He suggested the man take his eyes off his possessions and wealth. Ouch. You're teaching me a lot through stories like this—mostly, that I'm not my own savior. I am depending on You, God, not just to open heaven's door, but to get me through this life. Thank You for doing what I couldn't do for myself. I'm eternally grateful, Father. Amen.

Be the Change
Make a list of all the things Jesus has done
for you that you could not do for yourself.
Share your list with a family member.

SOW IN TEARS

They that sow in tears shall reap in joy.
PSALM 126:5 KJV

A farmer plants his seed in the ground knowing he will one day reap a harvest. Something kind of like that happens in my life when I go through sad seasons. It's almost like every tear drops to the ground, is planted, and springs forth as a little joy-plant. Sad turns to happy, just like that! Only You could do this, Father. Only You could take pain or a broken heart and turn it into a celebration. Only You could remind me that it will all be worth it in the end. So the next time the tears come (and I know they will), I will do my best to remember that they will turn into joy if I don't give up. Thank You for this reminder, Father. Amen.

. . . .

Be the Change

Write down the story of a time when you came through a sad season that ended in joy. Use your story to help a sad friend.

THIS IS ETERNAL LIFE

Now this is eternal life: that they know you, the only true God, and Jesus Christ, whom you have sent.
JOHN 17:3 NIV

There is no eternal life without You, God. No one enters heaven's gates without coming to a saving relationship with Your Son. That's why it's so important that I let people know. It's not enough to wonder if people are ready for heaven; I have to know for sure. I've got to tell them—somehow, some way. I need to share Jesus with my family, my friends, and my neighbors. Show me how to do this. I'm just a kid, but I want You to use me. Give me chances to share what You've done in my life. I will proclaim Your goodness, Lord, and watch You move. Amen.

. . . .

Be the Change
Offer to help your neighbor with a difficult task.

ETERNAL PRAISE

*The fear of the L*ORD *is the beginning of*
wisdom; all who follow his precepts have good
understanding. To him belongs eternal praise.
PSALM **111:10** NIV

I love worshipping You, Father, whether it's through song, prayer, Bible reading, or shouting Your name. When I think about what worship services are going to be like in heaven, I get so excited. Sometimes I like to think about what the music will sound like. Are the world's best writers already composing new melodies? Are some of the best singers warming up their voices in preparation? What will it be like to have the finest musicians, the most amazing singers, all together in one place, leading us out in heavenly chorus? I can hardly wait to see (and hear) it all for myself. Amen.

Be the Change
Invite a friend over to sing Bible songs.

ETERNAL PERSPECTIVE

*For since we believe that Jesus died and rose
again, even so, through Jesus, God will bring
with him those who have fallen asleep.*
1 THESSALONIANS 4:14 ESV

It's hard to think about death sometimes, Lord. I get so focused on the people I've lost that I forget what an amazing time they are having in heaven. I wish they could come back and visit, but they wouldn't trade heaven for anything! So I won't wish my loved ones back. I'll let them go to You. Instead of focusing on how I feel, change my thinking. Give me teeny-tiny glimpses of what they are doing in heaven. Singing? Worshipping? Getting to see people they haven't seen in years? Oh, I can hardly imagine, Lord, but I'm sure it's glorious. Thank You for taking care of those I love! Amen.

. . . .

Be the Change
*When your friends and family miss loved ones
who are gone, remind them how much fun
their loved ones are having in heaven!*

THE GIFT OF GOD

For the wages of sin is death, but the gift of God is eternal life in Christ Jesus our Lord.
ROMANS 6:23 NIV

Salvation is a free gift, one that I'm eternally thankful for, Lord. It cost me nothing (except my heart), but it cost Your Son everything. You've asked that I share this gift with others. . .and I'm trying! Sometimes in the moment, I freeze up. I can't think of what to say. I haven't memorized the verses or worked up the courage to speak up. That's where You come in. Your Holy Spirit energizes me, reminds me of all I've received in my own life, and gives me the oomph that I need to share my own personal story with others. Before long, they're ready to receive that free gift too. Salvation truly is the gift that keeps on giving. Praise You! Amen.

. . . .

Be the Change

Memorize the Romans Road (the verses in Romans that speak of how to be saved). Then you can use it to help you share the gospel.

IN MY FATHER'S HOUSE

"In my Father's house are many rooms. If it were not so,
would I have told you that I go to prepare a place for you?
And if I go and prepare a place for you, I will come again and
will take you to myself, that where I am you may be also."
JOHN 14:2–3 ESV

Oh, how I love this scripture, Lord! It gives me a picture of heaven and makes me feel like I already belong there. Jesus has already gone to prepare a place for me. This makes my heart so happy. It's like when my parents prepared my nursery before they brought me home from the hospital. They painted it pretty colors and filled it with stuffed animals. I'm loved. I'm accepted. I have a place prepared just for me, with all the things I love. You're going to personally escort me to this home, Lord. That's the biggest blessing of all. You'll be with me every step of the way, welcoming me through the doorway, arms open wide, tears of joy in Your eyes. I can't wait to spend eternity with You, Lord. Amen.

Be the Change
Read everything the Bible has to say about heaven so
that you can share what you've learned with others.

FROM ETERNITY TO ETERNITY

*"From eternity to eternity I am God. No one can snatch
anyone out of my hand. No one can undo what I have done."*
ISAIAH 43:13 NLT

Father, sometimes I like to think about what You were doing
before You ever created mankind. I try to imagine it all—before
stars, planets, rivers, and mountains. Before animals, plants, or
sneaky snakes in the garden. Before morning, noon, and night.
If I'm being totally honest, it's too much for my mind to understand. If I believe in eternity (and I do), then I have to believe
that there was no beginning and there will be no end. You always
were. . .and You always will be. You were present before, You are
present now, and You will be present for all eternity. And best of
all, You loved me then, You love me now, and You'll go on loving
me forever. Thank You, Lord! Amen.

. . . .

Be the Change
*Pray that all the people you know (and those you
don't) will get to spend eternity in heaven with you.*

SCRIPTURE INDEX

OLD TESTAMENT

NEW TESTAMENT